THE *Simple* LIFE

MARTIN KARI

Copyright © 2025 Martin Kari.

All rights reserved. No part of this book may be reproduced, stored, or transmitted by any means—whether auditory, graphic, mechanical, or electronic—without written permission of both publisher and author, except in the case of brief excerpts used in critical articles and reviews. Unauthorized reproduction of any part of this work is illegal and is punishable by law.

The short stories, in particular the fable samples, are entirely presented in the author's own version while a few of them are the author's own creation .

Subject Category: Philosophy & Ethics, Sociology, Short Stories

ISBN: 978-1-63950-333-9 (sc)
ISBN: 978-1-63950-462-6 (hc)
ISBN: 978-1-63950-334-6 (e)

Because of the dynamic nature of the Internet, any web addresses or links contained in this book may have changed since publication and may no longer be valid. The views expressed in this work are solely those of the author and do not necessarily reflect the views of the publisher, and the publisher hereby disclaims any responsibility for them.

Writers Apex

Gateway Towards Success

8063 MADISON AVE #1252
Indianapolis, IN 46227
+13176596889
www.writersapex.com

CONTENTS

About the Author v
Dedication vii
Acknowledgements..ix
Back Cover Blurb xi
Prologue...xiii

Chapter 1   Collecting as Much as Possible in Life..................1
Chapter 2   Having Few or No Possessions 4
Chapter 3   Rich vs. Poor 9
Chapter 4   Working Hard to Gain the Simple Life..............25
Chapter 5   Relaxing or 'Lazybones' 30
Chapter 6   Staying on Good Terms with Success................36
Chapter 7   Turning the Cold Shoulder on Success..............43
Chapter 8   Being Strong and Healthy.................................49
Chapter 9   Being in Need of Help 53
Chapter 10 Staying Honest or Grappling with Dishonesty....69
Chapter 11 Ignoring or Respecting our Fellow Creatures 76
Chapter 12 Embarking on the Righteous Side of Life..........90
Chapter 13 Taking Advantage of Evil Practices 97
Chapter 14 Being Endowed with Talents and Intellect 106
Chapter 15 Sharing Life with Less Gifted Individuals........118

Chapter 16 Living a Hermit's Life 127
Chapter 17 Following the Life of a 'Jack of All Trades' 144
Chapter 18 Helping Other People 152
Chapter 19 Leading the Life of an Egotist 162

Epilogue 169
Appendix 171

ABOUT THE AUTHOR

Born in Transylvania during World War II, Martin Kari's life followed many pathways, starting with his time as a refugee in Germany. Technical and then formal higher education prepared the author for life with a sense of exploration, adventure, intellect and humanity. Having worked and lived on four continents as a global citizen, he settled in Australia with his wife and six children. It was only in retirement that he found the time to take up the pen again, proving that it is never too late to take on something new in life.

DEDICATION

To my beloved wife, **Arja Kari** —

You were my constant light, my greatest friend, and the quiet strength behind every word I wrote.

Your love filled my days with warmth and gave my dreams a home. Even though you are no longer beside me, your spirit lives within every page, every story, every hope I've ever shared.

This book is a reflection of the simple, beautiful life we built together — a life shaped by your kindness, your laughter, and your unwavering love.

Your memory will forever be my compass.

Always and forever,

Martin

ACKNOWLEDGEMENTS

My thanks go here to a dedicated and open-minded team of the publisher , and my local editor Karen Mackay , who all helped to bring this book to publication- stage .

BACK COVER BLURB

If you are looking for 'simplicity' in life, here is one direction to follow. In this book, the author shows, through exploring real-life individuals and fairytale characters, additional paths to follow to acquire "The Simple Life." 'Simple' is by no means tantamount to 'easy'. On the contrary, it is only because of careful observation and sensible practices that 'simplicity' can be obtained.

Here the author aims to connect with the 'ordinary citizen' through a shared understanding of many of life's challenges, using common sense and therefore not needing specialised knowledge. The author also believes that we all have much of this knowledge stored somewhere within us, waiting to deal with various facts and discussion points which will either confirm or question many aspects of our day to day life.

A search for 'simplicity' in life is not something new. Religions, traditions and education have all dabbled in the subject without really updating their views with new insights gained from daily experiences. Find out in this book how the author, Martin Kari, updates 'simplicity' within real life-situations by showing the positive pathways in life. The author reminds us also that, when stuck in difficulties, we wake up and long for 'simplicity'. Therefore, it is instrumental not to wait too long for such a wake-up call and not simply ignore a well-intended advice. 'Simplicity', after all, is the key to everything in a successful life.

PROLOGUE

Where is the answer to achieving the 'simple life'? It is only by recognising the opposition to what we are doing that we become aware in which direction life is travelling, whether it be a difficult or an easy pathway. As we move through life, simplicity is discussed from every angle. However, it is much more difficult to achieve. So how is it that difficulties – those oppositions to simplicity - establish themselves with committed tenacity in our lives? To find the key to a simple life out of all life's complexities is by no means a straightforward undertaking. This will be neither the first nor the last attempt to shed light on what makes a life 'simple' and why it is worthwhile pursuing this goal.

Generation after generation have questioned life, looking for its 'simplicity'. Such a continuous questioning in real terms is called 'practical philosophy'. Through a constant dialogue, everybody contributes to a wider awareness of all the issues concerning our lives and eventually what may follow it. It needs also to be said that just because we are pursuing a simple life, it does not mean all our longings will come to an end. We can only follow that 'track' by constantly pursuing a simpler solution out of the overwhelming difficulties we sometimes face.

Doesn't the grass always seem greener over the neighbour's fence? The fact that we seek confirmation of where we stand outside of ourselves is enough to drive us into the difficult territory of comparing our lives with others. We can only pursue simplicity in the closest possible encounter with our own life. A look over the neighbour's fence is always tempting, which demonstrates the difficulties of how to get there, while it is our own territory that holds the key for the simple answers. The one who moves over 'fences' onto 'greener grass' eventually accumulates wealth, but at the same time loses ground from where he/she came from. Stepping back, on the other hand, has never been easy and therefore the resulting wealth has become the power, which drives us out of our own territory.

On the contrary, staying idle in one place cannot be good either; it could lead to poverty. Where then is the ultimate path towards simplicity in life? There should be a balance of going after the greener grass, and finding ways to cultivate gains in one's own paddock in order to prosper. This way we don't get lost in an endless search for more wealth outside our comfort zone. In our own field, we are better at doing what suits us rather than trying constantly to climb fences into others' properties.

What about the adage that life is never meant to be easy or simple? Aren't there two ways to look at this question? One view looks at the half-filled glass and optimistically sees all the water there, whereas someone else only sees the emptiness. Both views are valid but represent two very different outlooks on life. For one person, the half-filled glass represents an achievement while the other person sees the shortcomings in a half-full glass of water. Such opposite views can be regarded as relative to a person's life experiences.

In simplicity, a master is born within a restricted environment, which again is one of the keys to a simple life. Before investigating opposing life situations in order to collect arguments in support of the 'simple life', a look at the novel 'Robinson Crusoe' holds some clues. In the 1950s, the aftermath of the Second World War held Europe firmly in the grip of hardship. No future better times had appeared on the horizon yet. A struggle for daily life left enough room for fantasies, as described in the book, to be born in an escape from an uneasy reality. In 'Robinson Crusoe', somebody had found an escape from the ups and downs of life's realities.

However, as the book brings out, this escape from civilisation first happened accidentally, as everything else in life does. Here the idea of a 'simple life' was not planned but recognised and consequently taken on board. This idea is representative for life-situations as they happen to us, begging for decisions to be made.

Without going into too much detail about the book, delivering the 'simple life' away from the current civilisation, proved a challenge for the protagonist in so many ways. An escape from the deserted island on which he was shipwrecked challenged Crusoe's abilities. The 'simple life' he had found on the tropical island, away from the demands of civilisation presented its own challenges - sacrifices, risks, unknown occurrences and much more. It does appear that no life situation comes without certain challenges, the only difference being that it is up to each individual to find a way through the maze of life.

Individuals are, as the term indicates, particularised, so that no single obliging rule can be found for everybody. Each 'individual' has a different understanding about the same life issues, especially when it comes to decisions of a personal nature like pursuing the 'simple life'. What appears simple for one however, is not necessarily perceived as so by somebody else. A simple feat for one person might be a difficult one for another individual.

Let us find out how eventually to attain a 'simple life' by highlighting reflections on life and determining from there the avenues that lead to such simplicity. However, before this question is studied, another raises its head. Is a 'simple life' actually the preferred option over a more difficult one? One response could be that it is only when an individual meets difficulties that he or she longs for the opposite - simplicity. Rarely is 'the forest seen for the trees' unless we are actually in it. It remains with us to make moves to get there. The trees in the forest could be regarded as the evidence of life's simplicity, which in reality is there only to be recognised.

In life, aren't things regarded as 'simple' when they can be managed, whereas 'difficult' things call upon the limits of our capabilities through increased efforts? There is a balance inherent in every individual according to which 'simple' and which 'difficult' tasks receive attention first. Tracking life situations can demonstrate how individuals handle 'simple' and 'difficult' events by a different understanding, which leads to expectation-variations about a 'simple life'. Finally, we are all travelling on the path to a 'simple life', only varying in the distance to this goal.

CHAPTER 1

Collecting as Much as Possible in Life

John is a respected car dealer in a pulsing suburb of a major city, which could be located anywhere in the world. His father, who is now retired and watches over things from a distance, started the business many years ago. An exhibition room of shiny, new cars is located in the middle of the busiest section of town, in the neighbourhood of a large shopping centre and other community facilities.

Sales of the cars have continued to go well since John stepped into his father's shoes. A workshop was added behind the main exhibit building and, only recently, a petrol station followed on the side of the main road. This, with the inclusion of a fast food outlet and its own small shopping facility, turned the whole enterprise into a major business concern in the local environs. Everything appears to be going very well. Money keeps changing hands constantly and continues to help in expanding the business.

John is also married. His two teenage children fortunately receive attention from their grandparents because John and his wife are flat out every day looking after their growing business. In their minds, the money from the business easily compensates for the lack of time for other things in their lives. When time allows, almost everything is at their disposal. Things are going so well that money represents no problem anymore so that even the banks have been cooperative.

In fact, though, the children don't see their parents very often because business has become a priority in John's life. Everything revolves around money. Their two children however, have learnt how to get their share out of this success by pestering their parents incessantly. John and his wife always give in, buying their freedom from their own children. This doesn't stop with just their children as other people have also found out how to garner a fair share of this money tree. Time is only available for those who can appreciate and eventually contribute to the success of the business.

Naturally, not every contribution is strictly beneficial and the more the circle with other people widens, the more a rule establishes itself; not just wins but losses also have to be accounted for. Difficulties can now enter their lives as control has turned from a simple thing into a much more difficult one. Those who control the money were originally dedicated to business and family. Now there is the seduction of greater riches where money laundering is only a small step away. Success in one field can also encourage the test of fortune in new fields under the strong conviction that the road to greater wealth is only waiting to be travelled.

Almost predictably, activities outside the business become the norm: casinos, racing, flash cars that attract other female 'players'. As these women pursue their own wealthy lifestyles regardless of other 'players', trouble can begin in the marriage. Moreover, overconfidence has never served anybody well. It can lead to a downturn of commitments towards more sustainable, individual conditions. A downward spiral is never far away from a high-altitude flight.

Wisdom and life experiences can tell us that only so much of this sort of lifestyle can be maintained. Difficulties start when one indulges in more than any individual is capable of handling at a certain time. A simple life builds on a balance of want and possible achievements. Therefore, individual capacity is responsible for achievements in a simple life. What might be difficult for one is not necessarily so for somebody else and the same can be said of simplicity. Unease, worries, poor health and negative responses from fellow 'travellers' can often be the first warning signs of personal over-commitment. This can be the starting point away from a simple life.

CHAPTER 2

Having Few or No Possessions

After having circumnavigated only one of numerous stories of 'plenty' within an individual life, it is time to look at the opposite situation: an economically and socially deprived life. To find a representative case, it is not necessary to go far - just a step outside our usual environment.

A vast majority of people today still live in deprived conditions. We only have to look around us to realise that not everything that shines is gold. Could these lives somehow be regarded as simple lives? It is very unlikely. Therefore, let us look closer at those people with few or no possessions.

Instead of going further a field, it is possible to stay in the previously mentioned suburb. Opposite life-conditions can also be found in nearby neighbourhoods. It is not necessary to go away from our own borders to Africa, South America or some other third world country. We have only to become more aware of the environment in which we are living to find out where the shoe pinches other people. Social benefits cannot reach everybody who is in real need of help.

Not far from the car dealership, in a little backyard house, a young student couple live on the ground floor and a retired woman on the upper floor. The small premises indicate that neither tenant has many possessions. Still there are significant differences in expectations when time allows a closer look into each tenant's life. It is necessary to take part in the lives of both tenants to show how closely we can live in ignorance of each other's living conditions. Although these observations date back a number of years, I believe, they are still representative as this end of a society could never have moved out of their 'pinching shoes' quickly enough.

Looking from outside at both parties, it does appear that in one aspect they share common ground i.e. having few or no possessions. However, that's about all they share and vast differences still surface in their daily lives. Both parties live in rented accommodation with an inner court, which is surrounded by multiple storey tenement blocks, cutting out much of the natural daylight. The young students started under these conditions whereas the single, elderly woman has ended up here dependent on a less than adequate pension. More people than we are prepared to admit live in appalling conditions, often in a nearby neighbourhood. Does the world really have to be like that, divided into haves and have-nots?

On one side, the student couple could look past present restrictions in their lives to a future where their current educational undertakings will eventually lead to a better role within society, which in modern time they are told to aim for. At the end, they too will find out that they have to work this out on their own, as society won't do it for them. The elderly woman on the other hand, finds herself, along with many others, in a struggle to understand better where she stands in a world, which has changed, beyond her present comprehension.

Experiences out of her long life have almost become an obstacle in her life. Roles have changed from when she was younger into a difficult path through life's progress. Life outside accustomed routines appeared also for the elderly woman to happen in a restricted period of time. More people are left behind than a progressing party can take on board.

Does progressing in life also mean we have eventually to leave behind something we value at times?

The student couple, conversely, aren't much concerned about either the present or the future. It is the privilege of the young to spread their wings and see where their lives lead; it is a natural fact. Nevertheless, there is still more than one way to look at living conditions. People often living close together share very little in a modern demand for competition. This affects individuals with similar living conditions and is more than a mutual support system could deliver.

On their move into the one room accommodation on the ground floor, the student couple first experienced a grumpy, unpleasant housemate in the elderly woman who lived in the room above. "Again young folk who don't care about other occupants." Apparently, the previous young tenants who had moved out had continued behaviour of little or no attention for their fellow-lodgers. If this were to continue with the new tenants, it would be new grist for the woman's mill, reason enough for her to continue playing her grumpy role.

However, the small consideration of helping bring coal briquettes during winter up the steep staircase to the old woman's room, made all the difference. "You must be an angel; if you knew how it worries me going up and down this staircase with my stuffed-up old legs." The elderly woman almost instantly forgot about her isolation, joining in occasional conversations and a weekend highlight with a coffee-club, both parties taking turns to host it. All of a sudden, the little possessions lost their appeal, not weighing anymore on anyone's shoulders. Kindness and attention had played their role in interpersonal relations.

Whether it is a concern for the young or the elderly, possessions alone will never tell the truth about an individual's wellbeing in physical or mental terms, as said possessions cannot speak for themselves about how they came to exist. Their use as an identity status could be regarded as only human but 'isn't the whole point of life in doing things and not having things'?

Many are likely to see life in the way an automated dispenser waits for the coin to drop before releasing the 'goodies'. How to get to the 'coin' is more often the point. However, once the 'coin', a preceding remuneration for effort, has become available, discord can still surface between 'goodies' and 'owners'.

Hans Christian Andersen, the Danish storyteller, for no reason other than to prove the point of people's opinion over possessions, tells us the story of the poor peasant who didn't even own his land. No matter what the poor peasant tried to say, nobody wanted to believe one word he uttered. Only when circumstances changed and the poor peasant accidentally found a hidden treasure, did the tide of opinion amongst people suddenly turn, so that now everybody was listening to what the farmer had to say.

In disbelief of such a change, the farmer himself then tested his fellow villagers. No matter which lie the farmer produced, his words were still taken seriously even when he claimed that in the barn of his farm, which by then he owned, he kept one special mouse that regularly ate the stored steel bars. The now rich peasant thought, "What a load of rubbish by so many blind believers." When he had nothing, nobody was prepared to listen to what he had to say. Only now that the others could see his wealth of possessions, his words had the power over gullible fellow creatures to make them believe everything he said.

Here, as long as a majority of people are deprived of possessions, many would easily follow in believing what they see, especially in something they don't have. Only mind power can make people look at something with a degree of independent opinion. Moreover, how is mind power born? Basically, it comes from a mutual learning process with others, which personally is taken further.

Another reflection on possessions commonly popular with people is generated by an advanced social system, which in recent years indicates that most people have adopted a selfish attitude. They presume that everybody else too is covered against the shortfalls of life. How wrong this can be is evident the moment we step out of our accustomed life routines in order to spare moments of our precious time to support others.

Only then, when better observing and listening, will we very quickly find out that more is behind people and their situations than the eye can capture. The ones with few possessions are not necessarily disadvantaged. The attention people share, accounts for social wellbeing, which includes access to the many little individual concerns and not just a focus on the obviously bigger achievements. Life's 'building blocks' are all small in reality. Only when put together without 'blocks' missing can the 'bigger picture' eventually emerge, not much different from a puzzle.

Such a resulting balance in an individual life, where there is a correspondence between needs and possessions (no matter how few or how many possessions are owned) renders people equal in their wellbeing. A missing link to the sometimes hidden needs of individuals often is the cause for social differences reflected also in possessions. It is from this viewpoint that one can ascertain whether life's simplicity of few possessions can make up for the differences of those with plenty of possessions. This means, individuals with few or no possessions are in a sense not entirely disadvantaged as long as they receive appropriate attention from their fellow creatures.

In addition, it should not be forgotten that life offers many ways of compensation for shortfalls for the ones that become aware of it and seize a window of opportunity. Therefore, he who lives with awareness reaches satisfaction on the road to life's simplicity through having few or no possessions. Their lives are often better than the intricate roundabout lives of those who have plentiful possessions. 'Doing things, not having things, is the whole point of life.' With this understanding, possessions alone cannot help answer the big questions inherent in so many of life's issues.

CHAPTER 3

Rich vs. Poor

This is a question that everybody would like to answer with, "Yes, rich please!" What are the distinguishing marks of 'poor' and 'rich'? Both do exist and make for a polarity evident in all societies: no rich without the poor, but interestingly not the other way around, no poor without the rich. Why is this so? The poor can do without the rich, whereas the rich cannot exist without the poor. In fact, the poor have not much to lose if left alone, while the rich depend on others, including the poor, to help make them rich.

At all times throughout history, people have dreamed of becoming rich. Why has this been so? By looking more closely, one sees that society levels are identified mainly from rich and poor. However, when is that defining moment when somebody can be called poor or rich? The general public view about this may differ considerably from that of an individual's viewpoint. For instance, our modern status symbols of clothes and cars in connection with people as the 'possessors', induce many to consider individuals as rich or poor, because our dreams produce the pictures we use to compare ourselves with others.

The next question then would be, from where do such pictures originate? Is it advertising, education, or our own experiences forming the images of rich and poor? The more we know of personal experiences, the better we can compare ourselves with others regarding the status of rich or poor. Somebody driving an expensive luxury car is considered rich while the driving of a little 'squeezer shit box' doesn't necessarily indicate rich or poor. Both could presumably be considered contented individuals as both can move about with their cars. However, the fact that the luxury car cost considerably more money, points towards a difference in individual expectations, which still should result in satisfaction.

What about our human nature? The more we own, the more we want and one wish fulfilled will not stop new wishes from being born. This can become a never-ending spiral in our lives unless we can focus away from what makes us rich or poor. Such a focus could bring rich and poor closer to the so important satisfaction, which is a key indicator for a better society with better-balanced living conditions. The rich and likewise the poor aren't then made 'prisoners' in their own environment.

A less restricted vision on both sides keeps a dialogue open rather than contributing to a barricade between each other. Practical philosophy too is a key for life in order not to distant us from each other but to find ways towards each other. This may sound like just a theory; however, by incorporating a very practical side, it is rather another vital building block in the structure of a simple life. It is necessary to recognise that it is required to ask questions and constantly look for the answers instead of only accommodating set habits.

Early history lets us know in the bible that the rich will have the same problem getting to heaven as a camel through the eye of a needle. Modesty is what builds bridges between rich and poor and such a demand won't tarnish a rich person's glory in stepping down from their 'high horse' and meeting with the poor. We ought to be equal not just in legal terms; much more connects us to each other and this should not be forgotten.

The intelligent rich still stand on common ground with everybody else while their personalities do not enter into a dependency from personal achievements, which largely is responsible for the divisions in human relations. Ever since humans have aimed for something, divisions within societies became the result. Consequently new efforts were also born, individually as well as collectively, to minimise the rift between humans. How this happens is through endless ways of showing and modifying infinite directions.

The Greek philosopher Diogenes, who lived approximately 400 B.C., tried to overcome the number of controversies about happiness between rich and poor. To prove a point, Diogenes elected to choose absolute simplicity of life by living in a barrel with no material goods. Living up to total material abstinence, he developed his own understanding of a practical criticism of society's needs and conventions. His message for posterity was that we could only reach complete happiness by restricting the struggle for material possessions.

What would a Diogenes-based philosophy of living in a barrel look like today? "Here I am my own boss! I am not taking somebody else's place, nor do I compete with somebody else for it. Nobody asks rent of me, which is a considerable saving in my daily life. The worries remain with the ones that constantly rush past me, outside my barrel. I am staying in one place under a tree, a place just enough to protect me from too much sunlight with the barrel's shady comfort and shelter from the occasional rainy shower. The barrel also protects me from people's curiosity. Where are all those people heading that go past my limited vision out of the barrel?

Obviously everybody from outside is after something, giving an impression of a race in which nobody lets the other know either what the purpose or the goal is supposed to be. Outside there, people's appearances differ, from fancy fashionable clothing to 'glad rags'. Some wear more, some less, regardless of the weather, while my sackcloth takes me happily through the whole year. My barrel shields me also from the noise, which this outside world seems constantly to be living with. Whereas my own time and peace of mind give me plenty to think about so that I can find answers, not worries, to questions eventually turning up.

I am therefore never in a rush, because nobody can expect something of me, except myself. I can rest my mind and postpone what a moment cannot deliver. At nightfall, all this life around me slowly but regularly retreats into silence, which another awakening day leaves just as regularly behind, introducing to me the same scenarios of renewed noise and rushing populous. All this is spared me with my life in the barrel."

A Finnish fairytale tells about a boy who also lived in a barrel. His parents, in order to do something good for their child's future, followed the Diogenes' theories and put their son into a wooden barrel from an age as early as one year. They provided him with the little they considered absolutely necessary for him. Let us see where this simplistic life leads. After nearly half a generation's lifetime, the grown up son entered life outside the barrel for the first time, with the parents' consent, to find out how his past experiences would work. The main reason they let the boy out of the barrel to go into the real world was their insight that their son had to learn the existence of bad besides the good. Instantly caught by curiosity, the boy wanted to see for himself what life after the barrel is like.

The parents, right from the beginning decided also to provide their son with some cash so he could share in a way of life lived by everybody else. During his first encounter with his fellow-creatures, one in particular caught his initial attention. Still at home, he had received, along with his pocket money, the instructions to see the local priest - a black-dressed man with a white collar - about directing him to a shop where he could buy his favourite sausage. A middle-sized black dog carrying a distinct white collar-mark appeared on the footpath. The dog, mistakenly taken for a priest by the young man, must have been quite a clever one. On hearing the keyword 'sausage', the dog instantly remembered where such a smell had its home and led the boy there. The butcher handed over the goods for which he was asked. Money changed hands and back on the footpath, the dog took the sausage away from the boy's hand, disappearing in the street between a crowd.

Back at home, while facing the question of where the sausage or the money had gone, the boy said, "The 'priest' has the sausage but didn't give me any money in return."

"Tomorrow you'll see him again, because 'priests' are reliable and have money."

After so much was said and having returned to town where the sausage changed hands, the black dog with the white collar also turned up, hoping to receive another sausage. "No sausage any more", was the boy's answer. A request for the money was tabled instead, which a dog of course could not understand. The boy however was determined to get his money so he looked for somebody to help solve the problem.

A woman arriving at the scene clearly had this to say, "Somebody not paying is an offence which asks for a court ruling with the King." The boy appeared with the dog in front of the King to have the case judged. In the court was the King's family, including the King's daughter who lived her life quietly without any expressions of joy. Everybody in the Kingdom had heard of the award, "Whoever makes the King's daughter laugh will receive as much gold and silver as he can carry." In the assembly, the boy with the dog did not know what or what not to do. So he landed the dog on the floor shouting, "This priest hasn't paid me for the sausage I gave him yesterday."

Everybody present, including the King's family, couldn't help but fill the room with laughter and surprise. The King's daughter also laughed from the bottom of her heart for the first time. Nobody had noticed this happening before. The boy returned home putting the bag of gold and silver on to the parents' table exclaiming, "Here is the sausage money from the priest."

Another incident followed soon after in the new life of the boy who was brought up in the barrel. This time butter was the merchandise; the parents requested a trade for money. They felt the boy ought to start understanding money's circles with people. "Find somebody tall in town, well-dressed and looking down on you." Such was the instruction to send the boy on his way with the butter. Indeed the boy turned up in front of somebody tall of whom he didn't fail to ask, "Do you want to buy my butter?" No word came from the other side, so the boy concluded, "You must be deaf and dumb, but I will leave the butter with you anyway in the hope that it might help you."

In fact, the 'person' who received the boy's butter, was a statue on its own pedestal looking indeed from high up down to the boy. Back at home, the question for the money again hit the boy first which he answered, "The tall man didn't say a word, so I left the butter with him."

"Go back and find the man, give him a warning that he must pay for what he has received." The boy took it seriously, returning to town with a steel bar in his hand. To his surprise, the 'butter-man' was still there in the same spot. When the boy's strong demand for the money still did not receive a response, the boy got stuck into the pedestal bottom with the steel bar with the intention of shaking up the 'butter-man' properly. Instead of an answer, underneath the pedestal a shiny small box showed up, which on closer inspection revealed some brilliantly golden coins somebody must have secretly hidden there. Back home the parents were simply stunned when the boy spread the gold on to the table again claiming, "Here is the money for the butter."

Can simplicity such as this boy's early life ensure we find gold? Alternatively, is it that luck in life looks mostly for its equal? Could we all restrict ourselves to a barrel-life in order to find out what eventually makes us happy? Most certainly not! Nevertheless, the message obtained out of an absolutely consequent life is to discover truth in its pure form. Somebody has always to do the hard work to find the underlying cause of something from where others can learn and benefit. No society could however live a barrel-like life, but Diogenes can show us a life outside a barrel, too, even when we understand only part of his insight as long as we do not cut ourselves off from listening to what others have to say and to learn from this.

Let me tell another fairytale story as no other way can make us think in such an 'unburdened' light. The only reconciliation between rich and poor has become a discovery of simplicity in the fairytale, "The lucky person's shirt." The reigning Monarch of the Kingdom had been sick already for the most part of his life. Magician, witch doctor, non-medical practitioner, not to forget the priest, had all had their say on their ruler's deteriorating health condition. Nothing seemed to work so that other citizens were finally questioned too on the health of the Monarch. When everybody had almost given up on finding a cure, a seemingly insignificant peasant suggested to the Deputy Ambassador that the only cure for the King would be the shirt of a happy person.

Back in the castle when the message reached the King, the decision was made to send the King's personal deputies into all parts of the world in order to find the shirt of a happy person. Not long after and not far from the castle, a peasant was found in a field happily singing and laughing while picking the weeds. This must be the happy person, everybody became convinced, because who would otherwise smile and not worry when doing a job like weeding the fields by hand. The King was quickly informed of this discovery and ordered his support panel to see the happy peasant again. On arrival at the field, it was discovered however that the happy peasant did not even wear a shirt. The King, too sick to join the hunt, was confined to his bed.

So everybody returned to the castle empty handed but with a message to think thoroughly over what the meaning of the happy person without even a shirt constituted for them all, including the King. The more we have, the more worries we nourish and what makes one person happy cannot be simply 'lent' to somebody else. Everybody has to pursue and find the path to a simple life for himself, sometimes with the help of others. Much in life, we can borrow or buy from others, but not happiness.

Prior text has not established a stereotypical archetype for 'rich' or for 'poor'. It is by far too complex to reduce such terms to a single formula. A few samples should give a taste of the diversity of the rich and the poor. Before distinctness between rich and poor develops in life, which of the young teens would not go through stages of marking the pros and cons in a search for a life direction? All kinds of dreams prepare us from early age for moments to grab opportunities. We might be drawn into becoming a fast train driver, a movie star, a pilot, an ice-cream man, a bookworm, an astronaut, a postal worker, a boxer and so forth. Let us not forget that we all more or less go through developmental stages in life depending on guidance and support. The accidental constellation of so many other facts surrounding us should not to be underestimated. However, when facing life's realities, our dreams are constantly tested as to whether or not they can stand up to the challenges.

In today's world, increased competition is unleashed as greater numbers of individual interests meet on a collision course with individual numbers. Such opposition to our own cause compels us, at any stage of life to step back from our expectations by seeking refuge in a simple life. Challenges and how to deal with them are reduced to an individual's capability. The ones that do not want to, or cannot, step back are the fighters who wittingly or unwittingly can start conflict if not war. In the process, people usually find a niche in their lives, ability-tailored ways to rich, less rich, eventually poor with all possible stages in between. Simplicity then has become an individual's happy means between poor and rich.

In order to gain a better account of a simple life, real life situations can only help towards it. Let me start with the very rich person. Everything one could think off, he has achieved and owns. This is what people from around, everywhere, think by themselves and relentlessly reaffirm him. In fact, this rich man not only owns what most could only dream of, he has also everything at the tip of his fingers; a driver drives his car, the big house is maintained by a number of servants, garden and everything else is being looked after. The wife too has nothing to do; their children live with a caretaker away from home receiving every so often, when time allows, the rich parents' visit in order to keep up appearances. Everything is on hand; asking for it is all that is required.

How simple does such a life turn out? Hasn't everything a second side to the shiny medallion? Here the other side hardly becomes visible for an outsider: doing nothing brings along different pain than a lack of possessions do. Health is a measure of life-quality equally for the rich as well as for the poor. Our comfort through laziness only makes us rusty. Servicing 'rust' has always been a privilege of medical professionals, which the 'yes-men' in the proximity of the rich usually cannot easily recognise. Therefore, they miss every so often their visits through the hidden 'tradesmen's entrance' unless the rich have to see a hospital for themselves.

Money of course can provide care but still keeps the rich dependant on medical help, too. The time we save with the services of others, is used up somewhere else, not necessarily for a healthy benefit. Do we really save time, or does something else fill the gap instead? Simple tasks in life are often overlooked for the sake of so-called higher tasks, which lead us into conflict territory with others, more likely of a political nature in its widest sense. Where are the benefits of such a rich life? Hasn't quality of life been taken on a ride here, away from where we expect it and simplicity-compromised?

How are the poor on the other side dealing with life-quality and its simplicity? The poor people, knowing that they are poor, have reason enough that the others feel sorry for them. Therefore, to find the poor, we have to move out of our accustomed environment. Societies with a social welfare system in place for instance can at least reach out to their poor if their calls are not overheard. Little social welfare or none at all, on the other hand, isolates the poor in their own environment. Poor is where there is no hope; and to hope, one needs other knowledge than that which he/she is living with. Again, knowledge in isolation keeps hope in isolation, too.

Today's situation is that nobody really knows how many poor still live on earth. By counting not only the deprived in terms of living standards but also all shortcomings in people's expectations too, the world risks becoming in the future, a home for the majority of the poor. The percentage of poor must however be frighteningly high as if all these 'universally' classified poor have in the past represented a 'constant' in societies and still cling to it as the rich do by resisting change. People's discontent within a society, the result of shortcomings in expectations, has in reality become a new branch of the poor in a recently prosperity-driven world, which could be seen as a balancing act between poor and rich.

One visible first sign of an affiliation to poor is conveniently declared by a lack of possessions. Such a view however should be classified as superficial as many less obvious characteristics stand for poor today. For instance, the eyes of a person can often speak enough to the one who can read it, signalling a call for help but more often disappointment too while other appearances of the poor person could be anything that is deplorable.

At least, we have found a name for all these differences, calling it the 'poverty trap'. The question to answer here would be, "Who are the trappers?" There is no need to point fingers, as the trappers have only to remove traps. Otherwise, the chances for the poor to be freed remain dim once such a deplorable status continues its slides into even more deprived stages. The remaining quality of life follows the poverty trap, likewise health into frailty.

Trying to find simplicity exclusively with the poor, cannot be justified. Simplicity is based on the individual's minimum living conditions, which ought to be recognisable in a general individual satisfaction. Simplicity in other words, also asks for efforts to satisfy at least minimum needs. Making no effort whatsoever, whether unwittingly driven by circumstances or a lack of will power, is a direct road into the poverty trap.

a) The intelligent rich versus the intelligent poor

Intelligent has to be understood here in its original meaning, deriving from the Latin 'intellegere', standing for 'comprehending'. This is already one step ahead of 'learning' so that the intelligent poor, likewise the rich, can both be considered to have managed a learning process enabling them to live with an understanding of their own lives. As long as 'learning' doesn't lead into a comprehension, an individual reflection, poor and rich, live with much controversy. Whereas comprehension can lift both above their life situations onto more commonly understood ground. Poor and rich then no longer live in isolation to each other as they have found this common ground in simplicity, each one managing to come to their own conclusions about life's irreconcilable differences.

The rich are not caught anymore in mountainous problems related to possessions nor are the poor in a lack of it. Both have found simplicity in reconciliation with their own controversies, which are a focus away from given realities. The rich, for instance, can live in a busy, dense environment in order to exercise better control over inherent interests, finding the balance in an escape on a weekend into nature's forest during a silent, relaxing hike in the company of like-minded people.

The same catching-up with yourself can happen during another outdoor activity on an ocean beach, fishing, and sports but also with reading a book in seclusion. Numerous possibilities are available for us to focus away from what we do for a living by balancing those demands in a somewhat different focus, an easier and therefore simpler one. People who endeavour to balance their activities through simplicity in life are better societal partners with others, including the poor.

The poor, of course, balance life differently from the rich. They are dealing with different forms of life stress. Comprehension preceded by an individual learning process on one's own life situation should resume in a focus away from given realities, which the path to a simple life is also for the poor. Focussing away from life's difficulties means looking past restrictions. In order to do so, knowledge becomes imperative. This will enable the poor to find a way also towards a sustainable simple life.

In the past as in the present, religion has given a helping hand in a mind-driven focus, but there are other more practical issues, too. There is no objection however to philosophy as long as questions are asked and the answers can be found. Otherwise the practical little steps, representative of simplicity, can balance with contentment for the poor, too, in due time. Such steps could be the assistance for self help with tools and not with handouts, to work a field, conserve water, help create housing, establish hygiene, ensure provision of clothing, provide the necessary steps for an education and, last but not least, to seek any activity which helps towards more independence.

Once minimum living conditions have been established - which depend on individual expectations - a focus on simplicity is more likely to find its way. If all people however kept constantly raising their expectations, simplicity of life would be lost together with contentment. Possibilities remain that the poor feel rich while the rich feels poor, all depending on a simplicity-focus. Here, and only here, rich and poor can share common ground: the one who balances his life with simplicity rather reaches contentment in life. On a path to simplicity, we all are bound to find out, rich as well as poor, that to reach simplicity in life will take its own time. As we preoccupy ourselves with everything, life becomes complicated in nature before we learn to break things down to a more simple way.

On another note I'd like to quote a widely held common perception which generations appear to follow: 'Little children, little problems – bigger children ...' At times, parents are not spared having to listen to a new generations' opinions, "I don't want to become either rich or to follow your life; you've stuffed up the world. Moreover, it is we, the younger ones who you ask to deal with the problems that emerge out of it. I am happy instead with much less of what you have. For me it is more important to be happy with the little I want."

This is not an outburst of stupidity. Rather it is a sign of a way out of today's increasingly complex life-situations in a search for a more simple life. We all have at times during our lives sympathised with thoughts of a simpler life and where did we end up most of the time? It is probably somewhere in between a difficult and a simple life, driven more likely by circumstances from around us. Not many can draw a legitimate individual conclusion out of an encompassing life-polarity of simple and difficult. In fact, the more we aim for something, the more difficulties we face. On the other hand, doing nothing creates its own problems.

So it remains with every individual to 'differentiate' (recognise their own limits) or negotiate a life somewhere between difficult and simple according to circumstances, capabilities and comprehension. Simple and difficult will therefore range on different scale positions with every individual. Something simple might well be difficult for somebody else and so the reverse. The purpose of this book is to find a 'happy medium', which as a guideline towards a simple life can become a universal answer to all individuals.

b) when being rich becomes a 'crime'

First, when can somebody be regarded as rich - when he/she has accumulated more possessions than a single person can gain solemnly with his/her own efforts? So what is good or bad about being rich? It all depends from which angle you look at it. Whether rich or not, we all have come across rich people sometime in our lives. The rich live in a more exclusive environment of their own creation than the so-called poor do.

As an independent observer belonging to neither the rich nor the poor camp, I consider myself lucky to stay on good terms with a 'simple life'. Therefore, I see myself as an independent observer being able to establish certain typical behaviour patterns with quite a number of 'rich people'. Many of the rich are self-protective, suspicious, rarely straight forward and always weighing their advantages against possible disadvantages. Even during my time in a later period of life, I remember hearing during a meeting with influential, wealthy people such remarks as, "If I was born rich, life would be so much easier instead of having to battle a way to where we would like to be."

Where do you position yourself with the 'working class' and the so-called rich? Aren't the rich the ones who create the possibilities for the poor to escape their 'straightjackets'?

Again, who is right and who is wrong here? To tell the truth, I couldn't commit myself to an answer, rather remaining an observer as a Chinese wisdom symbolically suggests, "I do not see, nor speak, nor do I hear." This seems to say that we can never be completely sure.

The statement of a 'life-battle' in itself can be controversial as not only the rich makes this statement but also everybody else has a battle of his/her own in life, without exemption. Who in reality are the judges of the bigger or smaller battles? Isn't it only human to see the grass past one's own fence as greener or referring directly to a life-battle, the other is always better off because of a lack of clear vision. This occurs with people living in isolation from other realities, wanted or unwanted. It is here where crime can set foot, in disregard of other people's need, which becomes evident with the stereotypical rich person who finds himself isolated with almost everything he/she has achieved.

As long as the 'have' and 'have-nots' live at a distance from each other, necessary exchanges have a lesser chance of actually leading both parties out of a peculiar isolation. Not to remain in isolation, whether as poor or rich, requires an open approach towards all the societal groups not excluding the ones between the rich and the poor. A realistic understanding of the other sides in a society is a pre-condition for an improved coexistence with others. Then 'crime' won't have the upper hand.

c.) does 'crime' call home also with the poor

I doubt a figure on crime is available expressing a percentage of society's involvement regarding the rich or the poor. Then again, where rich and poor starts, is anything but a clear division. Internationally it is suggested that a minimum daily income is a measure for the poor. There are however, countless poor-levels in every society just as there are rich-levels, almost certainly never in a balance with each other. Poor and rich have always been antagonists surprisingly steadfast in their imbalance.

The actual emerging image of the poor is also relative to one's own life-experiences, which should culminate in an insight of this nature. Everything we experience could be worse. Many have seen countries in which big families are accustomed to send their children daily on a stealing-spree in order to bring home bare necessities for the whole family to survive. For these kids, such a day has an attached homecoming rule: "A young age doesn't matter so much as long as they can walk on their own. Don't come back home without anything." What a life's school this is!

Of course, people under the isolated protection of a living standard can easily overlook this side of reality as long as they are not unexpectedly woken up in the middle of it. A day's events determine for the poor kid which action to take in order to reach the homecoming target. Desperation drives new experiences and becomes the switch between theft and crime. How much crime is in the action of a poor person who simply has the desire to live more reasonably? And in reality, how much goes on the crime-conscience of a public's convenient attitude against an inconvenient attitude of the poor?

Theft, robbery, crime, attempted or not, has a common link which triggers 'behaviour mechanisms' not inherent in juvenile delinquents.

Rather there are broad circumstances surrounding those other than the poor. History tells us also that neglect over time is one major contributor to crime. The poor in South Africa for instance were to a degree neglected under Apartheid, triggering the downfall of its political system. A suppressed personal freedom only waited then to explode into a crime wave under a newly chosen freedom mainly of the poor, on an unprecedented scale.

Resorting to crime makes the poor as well as the rich equally lose the simple life. Often with the difference, however that the rich, contrary to the poor, are motivated by an insatiable desire for power: to possess and control as much as possible while the poor aim to satisfy basic needs. Interestingly however, is that most people managing to escape from the poverty-trap are primed to follow in the footsteps of many rich by adopting a race-mentality for power and possessions.

It seems to be part of human nature to grab opportunities as soon as they become available. Such an advantage-race is mainly responsible for the society's levels in which winners and losers are the result, widely depending on individual acceptance. In order not to be exposed too much to the risk of the uncertainty to become either a winner or a loser, the simple life is the way out. In other words, simplicity is a happy medium for the poor as well as for the rich.

CHAPTER 4

Working Hard to Gain the Simple Life

A common premise is that working hard will get you somewhere. So, what constitutes 'working hard' and where exactly does it get us? Let us look at the 'hard' part first. Does working hard mean performing physical work until the sweat shows, or is it something else? The hard part of the work is more to be found in perseverance of what we do. This doesn't necessarily exclude working up a sweat, depending on the nature of one's work efforts. Surely a stonemason or a weightlifter is more likely to produce sweat with their work than a non-physical worker is. A bureaucrat, for instance, sees to organisational procedures on paper; a student participates in the knowledge game from behind a desk. What they all have in common when claiming to work hard, is that they work with a vision towards an achievement. They pursue this in order eventually to make a dream come true, to satisfy their own or others' demands and sometimes for no specific reason at all.

Money, however, is predominant in most minds, because it is, in our modern times, the best-known reason for our work. We receive money for work, more money for hard work. Whatever we do, we like to see some purpose connected to it. This seems to be a common understanding. Are there other valid issues surrounding work, too? For instance, when 'working hard', we should never forget that we are not alone in doing so. Actually, with everything we do in life, others can easily engage us in subtle performance races in which, as in all kind of races, fewer winners than losers will emerge.

Life in the 'real world', on the other hand, usually predicates whether we are winners or not. Neither school results nor certificates from others can determine it as strongly as effort-based work. When focussing on 'working hard', one should neither overestimate nor underestimate individual capabilities. It is here where the first hurdle usually takes place. The course of life will set straight, hardworking efforts in relation to said capabilities.

A good illustration of this point happened on my property. We decided to move a massive old stump of a rubber tree that had been cut down almost ten years earlier. What was left looked rather messy in the surrounding garden of orderly planted and maintained palms, mango trees and bushes of ti trees, bottlebrushes and hibiscus. Three members of the family took on the job with a pickaxe, handsaw, chainsaw, crowbar, shovel and a heavy sledgehammer. The remaining stump scattered in multiple trunks within a diameter of three metres and was still sticking out of the ground up to a height of one metre. This made it less than straightforward even for the chainsaw. The job was further complicated by the rubber tree's sap, which sticks to anything that is exposed to it.

As expected, the job turned out to be extremely difficult and dragged on with time. Virtually from the outset of the work, people made comments such as, "Can't be done. It's all too hard. Nobody can lift or move those pieces. Other people wouldn't do such a huge job." Although questioning the hard work, all three of us stuck to our guns and gave his best, even when bathed in sweat. In hindsight, the quote from a contractor, which came to $2 500 (without guarantee that the job could have been done completely for this amount), might have proved a healthy saving. In fact, the job took us four hours. Admittedly, the job was hard, physical, and quite skilled work. The skill came in when strength couldn't get us any further. At the end of the day, no more rubber tree stump spoiled the landscape of the garden.

What happened was that the goal to get the job done was maintained despite real temptations to abandon the project. Here, work became directly subjected to hardship, which even during a limited time is a good measure of stamina. Stamina is the challenge that goes with 'working hard' when wanting to achieve a goal. I purposely had chosen a physically difficult challenge because the connection between the job and the goal was simple, straightforward, and recognisable for everybody. This is not so much the case with intellectual tasks where access is limited mainly to insiders.

Nonetheless, working hard, no matter at what level has the benefit of great satisfaction once a goal has been reached. Difficulties along the way can only build satisfaction as long as the difficulties correspond to one's individual capabilities. Failure to have difficulties at a manageable level, leads to disappointment and eventually down the road of personal failure. This then often can become the first step towards the camp of the less fortunate poor.

'Working' and 'working hard' can often lead to a simple life, which commands a balance between individual capabilities and objectives. An imbalance hereon usually shows up in a deficit of success, which is the road away from a simple life. Satisfaction, contentment, pride, and respect, are all inherent in a simple life, too, albeit on a 'lower' scale of expectations in a more even distribution. Too much one-sided focus keeps other life qualities, especially those in balance with a simple life, out of normal reach, consequently creating the overhang of difficulties.

We all have heard of the wisdom, 'A master emerges out of restriction only, a restriction into too many unjustified expectations.' What does wisdom suggest in relation to 'working' and 'working hard'? Working hard can make sense only if a limited timetable is attached to it for achieving a goal. How often, however, are we sidetracked and rather continue through habit with the hard work because other powers over us have taken over. Freedom of choice should remind us ultimately that whether we embark on a simple life or a difficult one, we make the choice because those two choices have entered our consciousness.

During a lifetime, everybody is asked to respond to personal freedom as far as circumstances allow it. Wisdom can speak to us like a signpost, which shows the direction towards a destiny along a bumpy road, telling us the distance left to go. Whoever can read the 'wisdom' signpost is more likely to succeed in travelling a specific road. A direction is given, which can help to focus further on our destination, past a position we are in at present.

A goal then becomes helpful in bypassing expected and unexpected hurdles on said road. The goal helps by allowing us to project ourselves with mind-power to other, hopefully better horizons by overlooking present difficulties. Philosophy together with psychology can make a powerful instrument for the individual, which also enables us to find personal freedom in a simple life. In particular, philosophy encourages us to ask questions so that we can open ourselves to answers other than those we conveniently cultivate out of insecurity.

Let me add here other wisdoms in order to highlight the 'rich' and 'poor' in a simple life from another viewpoint. 'Whether rich or poor, love is the essential capital.' 'For that man is richest whose wants are fewest.' 'Doing things, not having things, is the whole point of life. Joy must come from what we do, not from what we do with the money from what we do.' 'I am not as smart as most, but I work harder, because I come from the school of hard knocks.' (R.M.Williams)

What all this is saying, is that so many life qualities do not derive from wanting to be rich or from being poor. It is the restriction into a simple life, which can give us freedom that is more personal. Life on the other hand seems to run usually in widely adopted patterns. While young, we expand our longings and with experiences gained, when time allows, our insight redirects us to more simplicity. In life, on one side stands 'no gain without pain', which asks for hard work too. However, life will teach us that we cannot relentlessly accumulate possessions, wealth, and importantly the resulting power, if not wanting to lose our appointment with life. Get prepared for life, but do not lose count of achievements. Halting life's races wouldn't necessarily allow us a recovery in looking back on what has been achieved and therefore make us lose an understanding of our said appointment. Then, we could as easily be hooked on focussing on other people's interests, which is a sure path away from a simple life.

To a certain degree, everybody is master of his/her own life. We want the 'ups and downs' of life under the supremacy of difficulties, so we should never listen to others nor stop to labour under illusions. The wake-up moments, which we all experience from time to time, are in reality the chances to catch up with what otherwise we would lose. What is the conclusion now of whether or not to work hard? The complexity of such a question regarding 'the simple life' already is an indication of why simple answers are the difficult ones. By using various points of looking at a topic, and highlighting a number of issues (issues of common sense) collected in writing, a broader understanding might be fostered.

To sum up, money cannot buy everything, especially happiness and the contentment of a 'simple life'. It rather can do at least this, to keep us miserable in comfort and almost certainly never in a balance either with rich or with poor. Poor and rich have so far always been antagonists, surprisingly steadfast in their imbalance.

CHAPTER 5

Relaxing or 'Lazybones'

The difference between 'relaxing' or devoting oneself to being a 'lazybones', basically is that 'relaxing' finds its justification in more than one life-situation contrary to being a 'lazybones'. For instance, relaxing can take place before and after carrying out a task. If relaxing, however, is the only side of the 'work-fence' addressed then the road to being a 'lazybones' has opened. Remaining however, on the other side of the 'fence' after having climbed it - or completed the task - is more likely to become the situation a pensioner finds him/herself in.

Relaxing, in other words, looks back on an achievement but at the same time prepares a future with suitable action if wanting to gain the benefits that relaxing can offer i.e. reconnecting to a positive outlook in life with renewed energy. Then we can speak of relaxing. A 'lazybones', on the other hand, looks into the future with little or no action on his/her mind. A propos relaxing, it probably has as many different forms as the activities one can pursue. Real relaxing is a change from what has been done during a certain period. The time, the nature of the activity and the chosen form of relaxation can differ from individual to individual, depending on a complexity of facts.

Some, for instance, choose to have a swim after a walk; others sit down to read a book as the way to have a complete rest. Whether it is a physical or mental activity, the individual decides whether to relax with a physical or a mental pursuit, any oppositional measure to the work activity. It might be as simple as a sleep, depending upon the circumstances in which an individual finds him/herself and on the state of health, mind or fitness. Whichever, it is important to regain either attentiveness, strength or both together. The individual understanding of relaxation can vary the same way as the measures taken towards it. Therefore, it is no surprise that people also choose to relax more than what eventually is needed. It is important to keep in mind, though, that it is only 'the rolling stone that gathers no moss'. To seek refuge in constant relaxation can lead to becoming a 'lazybones', which is likewise caused also by escaping from life's realities with its indiscriminate challenges. This can also lead to misjudgements.

Alternative lifestyles then often become the end of such a road if desperation doesn't first drive individuals into the negative territories of life or mental collapse. Examples of a hippie or gypsy culture in most cases only contribute to diversion from real life issues. Once on this road, it is only a matter of time before one finds out that no life is without challenges. Even the alternate lifestyles have their challenges and it remains with the individual to find out which challenges are better to live with, that of the reality of the majority of people or perhaps that of the minority.

However, only a consistent attitude towards either lifestyle can foster the so important individual balance of contentment and happiness. Attendant circumstances like drugs in the hippie lifestyle, for instance, are distractions from the core issues claimed in the name of a 'simple life' for the wrong reasons. Doesn't a simple life start and end where an individual finds the balance between reality and wishful thinking, whichever is best tailored to his/her chances? Life with few material possessions, as most alternate lifestyles advocate, still is one that carries responsibilities, albeit on a different level with reduced expectations. It is up to the individual to watch that they are not driven by circumstances to unwanted lower levels of expectations. This is mainly because a return to higher expectations leads on to the road of stiff competitive battles. By going down the road of lower expectations, one meets fewer barriers than on the way up, as the majority of people push their way through life from a lower level to a higher level.

Every society might potentially cease to exist if losing its broader 'lower societal level', which in reality brings the sacrifices and efforts that move it towards progress. If, however, a lazybones mentality lays siege to a society in large numbers, that very society is threatened in its efforts to make necessary progress. Too many 'smart' people have then found an escape from said sacrifices and efforts. Societies have in the past always become subjugated to cycles of rises followed by falls, thereby shifting the standing of a society incessantly towards somewhere else. This is only natural as nothing is meant to last forever in this world.

Let me simplify, by the use of a few examples, the essence of this discussion, firstly in relation to relaxation. A word is often used without the inherent knowledge of its meaning, which however directs us to a word's origin as it is used in real life situations. The word 'relax' finds its roots in the Latin word *laxare* meaning 'to loosen' and *laxus* meaning 'at ease.' The prefix 're' in this word is a call to come back repeatedly to it when its opposite, our commonly known stress, reminds us of it. 'Relax' therefore finds its justification or merit only when being born out of oppositional life situations in which 'uptight' eventually becomes a descriptor.

A bricklayer, along with many other professions, has breaks during a day's work for resting, food intake, a talk with others, sometimes reading or just having a snooze. All this can be a form of relaxing as long as it diverts from the previous work activity. Some will need more of a food intake, while others relax to regain some strength and mind recollection in order to continue or change activities after a break.

Much of the work we do doesn't simply stop after a day's work, because the more we have collected in a consumer-driven world, the more work is waiting for us in order to maintain these consumables. These can be a home or a car but also a friend, a family, or a hobby. To keep a balance in all this becomes a challenge between stress and contentment. Relaxing can here be a road to contentment, possibly to find a balance in seeing a movie, going for a walk, participating in sporting activities, going to the beach, helping within a community, listening to, as well as practising, music, or pursuing a hobby. It is better for the relaxation activity to be something other than what we do for a living. Overall, this can help with relaxation as long as we have control over it. Stress usually starts when we are going to lose control over a backlog of activities. Here again, the treatment can be the 'simple life pill', which is cutting back on personal expectations that we are having problems satisfying.

What about the poor and the underprivileged? They certainly aren't stressed because of greatly exaggerated expectations, but they can and do still suffer from stress out of desperation to control more of their own lives. Relaxation for the poor widely becomes a *fata morgana* (mirage) while they remain in a constant state of a stress caused by what is known as the 'poverty trap'.

What is on one side over-the top expectations, which call for relaxation, is on the other side - mainly that of the poor - an undermined relaxing in suspended expectations. By looking closer into such a discrepancy, it should signal that the ones who are engaged in collecting as much as possible in life are the ones who are mainly preventing others to somehow get out of the 'poverty trap'. All can find the key for real relaxation via the 'simple life'.

Having discussed relaxation, a lazybones lifestyle could be called the 'wrong' way of relaxing. However, what could possibly be wrong with relaxing? Where effort-driven activities have been eliminated and one is being called 'uptight' contrary to 'loose' and 'relaxed', a lazybones lifestyle has taken over. An occasional bit of so called 'laziness' however can work in favour of relaxation, again highlighting the need for a balanced medium in all we do. Doing very little for most of the time does not just add up to a bit of relaxing but to inherent laziness. Again, the individual is the one who decides on inactivity by having chosen, for a number of reasons, not to follow the mainstream into which they see so many others locked.

Somewhere between 'too much activity' and 'inactivity' can be found the 'simple life'. On the way to less activity, is it the 'lazybones' who will miss the boat of a 'simple life' by going past it much further towards inactivity? The reason for going down that road is most of the time related to the environment in which an individual lives, causing the individual to follow the path of the majority in a sheep-like way.

Most people tend to look at the typical 'lazybones' with suspicious scorn, often jealous of somebody who has the audacity to be different from the mainstream in which everybody tries to surpass each other with questionable and often unnecessary efforts. Again, it depends on from which side of society laziness is regarded. Obviously to keep away from mainstream challenges and leaving the 'hard work' to somebody else, has for some, always been an escape. The justification often used is, "Those others, tearing out their arms with work, also reap the benefits."

Such a discussion could continue no end but still cannot escape the fact that a community, no matter how small, can only live and prosper with a majority that is ready to tackle life's constant and varying challenges. Somebody has to deal with this side of life and it is only natural that a polarity develops: 'lazybones' establishes itself alongside 'active-bones'. As long as no disproportion offsets the necessary balance, they can coexist. However, 'active-bones' claim outright that 'relaxation' in order to keep away from 'stress' is the best 'road' to a 'simple life'. In other words, both elements of 'relaxation' and 'lazybones' have the capacity to come to terms with a 'simple life' if constant dialogue is upheld. This prevents both parties from becoming isolated, but only if that dialogue leads to renewed activity.

Let me add a fable to this discussion. 'The Hare and the Tortoise' sees the seemingly slow, relaxed tortoise winning the upper hand over the cocksure hare. In an arranged race, the hare hops on detours from the start, into and out of the designated path ahead of the tortoise. Overconfident, the hare pauses every so often and looks back to catch a glimpse of how far the tortoise has come. Once the tortoise has disappeared from the hare's sight, the hare imprudently takes a break with a snooze, showing off its superiority. At the end, when the hare wakes up, it realises that the tortoise has steadily surpassed it and is about to cross the finish line. Here, the tortoise has applied the right measure of relaxing when appropriate i.e. the end of the race, whereas the hare has wrongly relied on the perceived 'lazybones' i.e. the tortoise, becoming the loser. Slow and steady wins the race!

CHAPTER 6

Staying on Good Terms with Success

Who wouldn't like to be the one who basks in the glow of success? Performance and results usually bear all the hallmarks of a success. So what is success all about? Is it to be that hair's breadth in front of others? But for how long? Isn't it also useful to remember that usually there is only one winner but there are many more 'losers'? In a sense, the many 'losers' allow someone to be the 'winner'. Besides the success of a 'winner', are the others really 'losers'? In the original meaning of the word 'loser', not at all. Everybody who competes towards a set goal becomes a winner of sorts: not necessarily number one but certainly one of the unlimited winners who have met their goal by participating.

The number one winner is also the one who pushes furthest his/her limits and sometimes as a consequence can become the victim of unforeseen circumstances like overstressing his/her capabilities, physically as well as mentally. Often a result then becomes a behind-the-scene-struggle to 'digest' the number one success, something not commonly noticed by the public. Success is not only sweet but also more often accompanied by a bitter aftertaste. To come to, and remain on good terms with, success is a bit like gambling. One only knows after the success has been achieved whether or not it is likeable.

Success is also established in many ways. For instance at the casino's gambling table, talk is about success just as it is during a sporting event or at an educational examination. The differences in success emerge however from a sustainability point of view in which the building blocks of a success must fit a prepared person's construction plan in order to be carried further. If this is not the case, the misfit simply spoils being on good terms with success. Success can be obtained in many ways but to stay on good terms with it, often is a different kettle of fish.

How often does success get spoiled? The moment success is achieved is one thing; to carry it further as the expectations especially of others demand, becomes another thing altogether. Easy come, easy go and so it is with success. Failure to keep succeeding can set back expectations - one's own as well as that of others - more than missing out the first time. Erroneous expectations play their role. Only sustainable efforts can support a success while quick success is more likely to fade away with a lessening of efforts.

Here are a few examples to support this discussion. Changes to a racing car that aim to improve its overall performance takes a supporting team many days, claiming many night hours as well. All these efforts peak at the start of another competition when the driver takes his position to race to the finish line. The driver's own confidence receives the wider support through the team effort, a good deal of luck and not least the driver's skill, enabling him to bypass all the challenges and ensure success in taking pole position in the next race. Back to the drawing board has then become the order of the day. If there is no slacking off from further preparation efforts, success will again be achieved with the team making sure each team member stays on good terms with their overall success.

To not win the race will not necessarily bring on the 'bad terms' of disappointment. Inferior feelings should not mean giving up a foothold in the winning game, depending on whether or not one's own expectations fall short. The right measure of confidence should keep both the number one winner and the 'winners' in second, third etc on good terms with their success as long as a goal within reach was set and previous lessons have been learnt.

The rules applying for a race almost certainly can be translated into other activities. A student for instance, preparing himself with knowledge for his life, better adheres to the racing-rules if wanting to succeed and stay with it on good terms. To some readers such advice might sound strange, but ultimately, isn't surviving any sort of 'race' from its start, right through to an end, a winning performance? A race is commonly understood as being fair as long as homegrown efforts can back it up. All artificial performance enhancing leads to a short success. One's own 'physics' will pay back with the answer: you are forcing me, I am resigning. Success like this quickly turns into a defeat of one's own capabilities. A 'highflier' then has come down, often much further down than his/her inherent efforts would have positioned him/her relative to the others.

Where then is the healthy medium in the ambition for success? How can we ensure it keeps us on good terms with it? If we can, we venture, because of a knowledge that nothing is gained otherwise. Humans are by nature inquisitive, always wanting to push any limits further, which receive the seal of success. The exposure in the search for success however is the menace to watch! On the other hand, isolation from the mainstream can become the likely result that begs its own rules in which one still has to answer the query about how to cope with the lonely success.

At first, success is always sweet, while the conditions attached become the real challenge. Then one has to ask whether its integration into an individual life can become a new reality. Real intellect diverges on this point as to overrate or underrate a person's capacity for success. In addition, we have to acknowledge here that every individual person has from his/her birth an inherited capacity to respond to the challenges of life. Keeping within those 'boundaries' means staying on good terms with any sort of success, whereas overlooking said boundaries amounts to a move onto very personal, very shaky ground.

The 'simple life' transpires again here in a balance between 'want' and 'need'. Where such a balance becomes more naturally evident, is in dealing with children rather than with adults. Most children have the capacity to listen if the other side wants to be heard for collecting experience before expressing their own will, which is more adult-like. Children let us know, too, unmistakably when they cannot follow us any more, simply because of a direct link to their 'need' and not so much to a 'want'. Intellect displaces 'need' with 'want' in a growing adult, causing the rift between childhood and adulthood. In other words, it is simply more natural to adhere to 'need' which in return serves the individual better, regardless of age.

Success as we like to recognise it, including staying on good terms with it, probably has an unlimited number of forms. Somebody winning lotto is considered successful. So too is a small company owner who has, over many years, built on his and the company's success with small steps. The student climbing the knowledge-ladder up to eventual success is also recognised as a winner.

One rule however will apply for all of them: easy come, easy go. In regard to success that comes easily, success can also be lost easily. In the case of the lotto success, it is almost common knowledge that this sort of incidental success too often loses its accompanying good terms quicker than we are prepared to acknowledge. Success's blessings can turn into an aftermath of new problems if not steadily nurtured and laid down like a strong house foundation. A foundation carries only properly prepared 'materials' that fit a building.

The other two cases, the entrepreneur and the student, are more likely to remain on said good terms with success by not losing track of the diverse practical sides of life. 'Practical' here is everything that succeeds. In other words, success is a practical side of life, demanding practical outcomes generated in a practical environment. On the other hand any theory of success cannot include staying on good terms when said success remains in isolation without transpiring into the practical world. Equally, efforts that are out of balance with a person's capability ensure failure rather than success. Success does not follow enforcement.

Everything on good terms, including personal success, asks for a commitment to a life-balance without the exclusion of simplicity. Somewhere between difficulty and simplicity lies the key to success. One side alone cannot deliver it; to come to good terms with success we have to embark on the dual sides of difficulty and simplicity. There is also no single valid rule of how to get there. Despite guidelines to leading successful lives within a society, every individual has to find his/her valid rules, which lead to relative success on good terms with others, too. The reason for that is, circumstances vary constantly and individuals face these on top of an invariable, individual, genetic setting.

The aim here is not to make matters difficult to understand. However, it is useful to pick a piece out of the 'knowledge-box' in order to avoid conflict through unjust expectations. Knowledge can be a wake-up call but at the same time act as a stimulus for reassurances. No doubt, it has always been our natural predilection to make life complex and difficult. Therefore, it also remains for us to seek success on the road to the 'simple life' in its many conceivable forms.

The pop music phenomenon of Michael Jackson, who recently passed away, clearly shows where success can lead. He obviously did not manage to stay on good terms with success. No doubt, Jackson enjoyed the wide recognition of so many fans but his own efforts were in stark contrast to his materialistic success.

In today's world, we should be aware that interest groups or fans make stars successful. The 'lucky' one who has been chosen for stardom is likely to enter into conflict with his/her own personality. Once famous, one cannot disappoint anymore; the pressure is on from outside to continue to perform in order to satisfy the expectations of others and nothing less than lifting success to a new horizon will satisfy.

The 'bad terms' of success often sneak in with time, trying to catch up with what has been left behind, mainly in personal terms. In Jackson's case, he tried to catch up with a lost childhood and in the process lost his appreciation for money. It became a commodity in exchange for something either Jackson has lost in his life or tested his growing success to see just how much it could deliver.

'Money soils everything it touches!' This epigram serves for a comparison with the fact that everything comes from soil and must return to soil – 'From dust we came and unto dust shall we return'. Corruption from money therefore introduced the 'bad-success' terms with Jackson, in occasional highly questionable appearances and personal moves that brought almost everything down in his life. Then suddenly, he himself disappeared from the 'Jackson Show'.

It wasn't Jackson's drive for 'perfection' of understanding only but the temptation to let money and not his 'ego' decide how luck travels when cosmetic surgeons artificially changed his physiognomy. An element of the racial divide in America's society certainly played a role in such a decision to make these changes in order to satisfy the non-black section of society i.e. the section that predominantly ruled the money-game. Almost predictably, these 'bad-success terms' imposed on him from outside, deliberately or unconsciously, caused Jackson to fall into bankruptcy. A majority demand for a constantly upgraded 'Jackson Pop Music Show' pushed aside the early, lovely appearance of the black child Michael was when he started first performing pop music to earn a living with the family. What a personal loss this was! No wonder that his personality turned so eccentrically extravagant, especially during his adulthood.

His extraordinary search for a personal identity could not connect any more with his childhood when he was such a naturally beautiful black child. This was displaced however by circumstances from outside. Even late in his life, Jackson only escaped rejection by the public when he tried to reconnect to his childhood by inviting children into his life.

Nothing however stopped him from finally losing everything that he had gained. Time alone will tell whether or not his pop music will survive him. Other emerging stars will determine with their performances where Michael Jackson stands with time.

I am also sure that nobody ever seriously asked Jackson the question of how to achieve a 'simple life'. Was he also one of those who struggled in a confusion of personal likes, wants and perceptive power to see the lights in the tunnel of a 'simple life'? Ultimately, his human failings left him bereft. 'To err is human' and that's the way it is; the more we do, the more we err. Through our existence, we are bound to err; therefore, it cannot be avoided. All we can do is minimise the error and balance our activities with more insight and not with blindness.

CHAPTER 7

Turning the Cold Shoulder on Success

Where does this get us? In a search for a 'Simple Life', not very far either! A main stream in a society exerts an influence from which to escape into a more individual lifestyle is difficult. The ancient tribal sense of a belonging plays here its role in keeping individuals with everybody else in a check-line so that hardly anybody escapes from set-rules and put himself ahead unduly. Such a 'society-brake-system' is today still operational amongst Indigenous Australian Aborigines who by the way are the oldest continuously existing known human society.

Success in today's societies is most of the time somehow linked to many forms of efforts demanding also personal sacrifices more than just to be at all the time a yes-man in a main stream. Success, no matter how small it might appear to somebody else, is however vital for an individual's well-being, especially in a larger community in which not much else remains for an individual to identify him-/herself in an existence other than through any form of a success.

The ones turning away from such a success-doctrine are likely to slip into isolation. As a consequence, the no-action through a lack of efforts makes missing the crucial satisfaction of being able to look at something that owes its existence to own creativity. Again in doing nothing for the wrong reasons of a 'simple life' is to set also the wrong signals in a life, which is synonymous to 'turning on success the cold shoulder '.

What makes people follow a road away from success? From an independent observation point of view it is often either the one resigning from personal efforts for a number of reason or somebody who has arrived at 'ill-founded-convictions', sometimes simply too of having resigned from personal fate's mercy. A resigning from personal efforts often happens during stress-situations in which somebody just had enough with the way things turned out; whether related to overly high expectations or simply out of impasses to get out of a poverty trap for instance. Confidence-rebuilding and renewed efforts will then lead to a healthier engagement with success again, while ill-founded convictions on the other hand can move individuals away from success more decisively because of a conviction, which already has instigated a life direction.

Thus occurs when people often in their numbers connect from outside to a person convincingly superimposing ideas on individuals not aware that also they have become prisoners of ideological warfare. As soon as in such a process the own efforts have reached the seemingly irreconcilable differences of poverty likewise a resistance is lowered to personal 'failure', reconciliation with success becomes distant or is 'turned the cold shoulder on'.

In the light of what can happen to people, fate plays its role too. Somehow along our lives we all have to deal with the 'lows' as well as the 'highs' of life and in particular when the 'lows' ask for renewed efforts to move us out of a life's ebb. More by accident than anything else are we usually ready to face those challenges, may be for personal or invoked reasons which when out of resignation can then too unleash an attitude of 'turning the cold shoulder on success'. Health problems can predominantly affect a personal freedom of active choices, while unforseen 'bad luck' not only individually afflicted but also in company with others, brings success quickly to a halt. The longer such a situation leaves us in limbo allowing it to take a foothold of us, the more likely we also can slip into poverty. Indisputably a 'down-turn' as a matter of fact always takes less time if counter-measures cannot become effective rather than its opposite, an 'up-trend', which by experience reluctantly takes all the time for a re-building.

What are typical 'cold shoulder success turn-ons'? We all have encountered people mainly in denser populated areas conveniently disregarding on biased terms a "Hippie, beggar, layabout, vagrant, social misfit, dawdler, tramp, loafer, idiot, scamp, sometimes even criminal and much more. Isn't it also here that we rarely see what really is behind something? In a fleeting glimpse, people might give an impression, which depending on an individual personality or circumstances often will turn out as an unfair judgement.

Not only I remember from my early youth my conservatorium music teacher (Prof. Wehrle) being dressed in a greyish loden-coat which covered his shoes and a felt hat with a wide brim pushed deeply over his head so that his eyes just caught a glimpse from under the brim. The man, in a sense, didn't look like a respectable professor of a Music-Academy; he rather looked as if been short of almost everything so that somebody easily could have become lured into handing the 'poor-bugger' a little change of money as support and a sign of compassion.

Latest from the start of the music-lessons, the image of the professor established itself when music took centre-stage, were it in a lecture or in a performance of music instruments. A sparkling spirit then revealed a strong personality letting completely disappear any other impression except that of a commanding authority remaining however absolutely kind.

Decades later as I recall this time, I cannot but conclude from more life-experiences that this gentleman had managed to live the 'simple life' true to his personal conviction with a great deal of freedom from appearance-demands which in return gave him time and energy to pursue his important aspects of life, music. He too lived what he had to say making him a convincing teacher. By judging people, we need to connect to their 'inner-attitude' and not necessarily to the one that becomes visible.

My wife too told me that she had in Finland a professor on Old-Greek and Hebrew who, one day on foot on his way to the University, was stopped by the police and interrogated about his appearance in public. Also he had little concern about an appearance rather dressing up in a way that he considered modest and most of all practical if not plainly simple. Only on confirmation gained from a phone call to the University that he was a professor at the Abo-Academy, the police felt of a sudden embarrassed letting the gentleman continue his walk undisturbed hurrying to find excuses.

As these two selective samples show, not everybody conforms to people's stereo-type-images, which are easier adopted than from a distance cautiously examined for their real evidence. This wouldn't apply only selectively as all people tend to develop different images during the course of their lives. Camouflage seems to be the key word for an intelligent survival. The better intellect is more likely to dominate of which the 'better' is open for discussion. Nature, the mother of us all selects criteria of what we recognize as 'better' different from our perception. Thus putting an additional question mark on people's appearances by referring more to its endless possibilities rather than through anybody's fault.

The poor in this world for instance likewise people living on the border of a broader society-understanding are not necessarily the ones that have 'success turned the cold shoulder '.

Some of them might be caught in the poverty trap while others are content in a belief of their own choice for a 'simple life'. The ones having turned 'success the cold shoulder' also can recruit from all society-levels often surpassing their credentials with unjustified expectations consequently falling therefore short on their way to a 'simple life'. Innumerable forms of personal shortcomings are the result of today's on the increase mixed societies where many live nothing else than an undercover image maintenance. Any form of a success inevitably is bound to meet competition, its creator, in an opposition to others.

Is it this challenge in confronting an opposition, which engages certain people, however at the same time, makes others walking away from it and 'turn a cold shoulder'? What about the way a said competition is unfolding? The individual character responds here to his/her needs. However, it too is almost common knowledge that "money rules the world," therefore subordinating everything to its course. A 'lure' hangs up to a height only few can reach, which is the old human running-match. Not all follow such a seduction. A number of cunning people still size up their capabilities from an outright often realistic distance lending an ear to this money-dominance before becoming too closely involved with it.

"Money is said to soil everything it touches" by establishing a dependency-culture with people who indulge in money. The human touch indiscriminately shifts here the 'bugs', too, without warning. When money-soiling everything would mean that everything comes again down to earth, this would be just about right because in the race to success with money the question is not so much of how many make it but moreover where would the majority of left-behinds end up? Social responsibility is called upon here. Somebody 'turning on success the cold shoulder ' out of a firm conviction can be seen as a preventive measure towards what might happen to somebody who was left behind in a race to success. A wisdom however tells us: "The heart's joy is in action" (La joie de l'ame est dans l'action-French wisdom) which encourages action as heart and action activate each other visa verse.

A rule in life appears to be to keep acting as long as we live, because we never could possibly know what lies ahead nor about an outcome. Who is now right? The one hesitating or the one acting? In the end it is the individual's personal freedom to determine how far to go on the road of success and not the voice of others which creates the discord between a 'simple-life' and success. Whether to race for success or 'turn the cold shoulder' on it, depends on every individual how he/she understands and manages life. All our 'wants' will however result in a simple message: "I was richest when my wants were fewest."

CHAPTER 8

Being Strong and Healthy

First of all, what has strength and health to do with a "Simple Life"? Are they prerequisites, a supportive measure or both? In order to find an answer, it is reasonable to look into an opposite direction of often too easily taken for granted life-situations. While looking around us, we mostly see more of the shiny side of life conveniently missing images of the lesser shiny ones. It is here however, where to look for an answer, because little strength and little health restrict the individual to compete on similar levels with others leaving him/her in isolation from a main stream.

How much notice is taken of people that are preoccupied with living conditions other than those of a main stream? To be true, very little, generally speaking. And why is that so? It appears always the fault of the others to be in a less strong and less healthy situation. The rich, the poor, sometimes the unfortunate battle a situation, whether through fault of their own or induced indiscriminately from outside, all this wouldn't help a 'Simple Life' much in a pursue. Those cases are less likely to qualify for it as their personal freedom of choice is hampered in remaining preoccupied with their own reduced living conditions ; one could also say : running around in closed circles, not sufficiently able to focus from the own away to other living conditions.

Strength and health are here responsible for moving people in their lives, physically as well mentally and putting their own problems into new perspectives. When strength and health are not given facts, such moves cannot take place creating contrary to it a dependence, which is a point of discussion only in the chapter 9.) to follow.

One in particular important issue of a "Simple Life" is a relative individual independence of strength and health. They are the starting points of any further independence. Mental independence, which in real terms is a result of physical independence born out of strength and health, is a driving force towards a "Simple Life." A lack of strength and health slows down own initiatives towards any form of independence and creates therefore a distance to a "Simple Life."

Everything in a life is also relative, which means that a given strength and health can easily lead also to over-confidence which can make the individual lose proper control over a more independent life allowing problems to surface. Again, it is the balance of a bargaining power of what we got in store and can bargain in an exchange for a better or a loss. On the other hand, can a less fortunate individual with regard to strength and health maintain a "Simple Life" better from a will-power, which leads to mental strength than from insufficiently controlled physical power?

Maintenance of strength and health and their opposition in challenges can be found in daily lives in in-numerous examples. No matter at what stage in our lives, a maintenance of strength and health remains a complex issue in finding the appropriate balance, tailored to the individual, between building and maintaining strength and health. Sitting idle and not making much of a building effort keeps on one side low a risk-level however shifting a negative outlook on to health because we all have heard of the wisdom: He who rests will rust – or – a rolling stone gathers no moss.

On the other hand, the dare-devil we can watch in all sort of races, in challenges of almost everything we do by pushing the own and other existing limitations further. Risks then become a hidden agenda depending not any more only on an individual's capabilities but on many incidental, difficult to control facts intrigued most of the time from outside. He who stands up to challenges and is able to continuously secure the positive outfalls, eventually can secure a built-up on strength, then on health, if the own 'physio' has not bypassed a health construction.

Do these challenges have room in a "Simple Life"? Very little, if any! No matter how challenges may turn out, they register on individuals' accounts differently than that of a "Simple Life. " It all comes back to a balance of activities which can maintain as well as build on 'being strong and healthy'. Indeed it is a prerequisite and to an individual degree a supportive measure for a "Simple Life." The emphasis here is on a balance of neither too little nor too much physical activities in order to allow our brainpower to catch up with it for a control of a "Simple Life." Anything departing from such a recommendation is doomed to failure in aspiring simplicity in a life.

Early history documented already in the "Old -Testament" the story of "David and Goliath." Let me here recall in a concise form this story in order to show that human society has always been concerned with issues of strength and other related issues. The 'small' winning over the 'giant' is a dream as old as humans can document history. Already before the birth of Christianity, the 'Old Testament' narrated an event in which 'little' and 'giant' played their role however in a context that was related to early religious believes. Today in the Second Millennium, people's understanding has considerably changed with fast interchanging information technology. Here is one reason to update a past understanding with a more present one, which I'm attempting in this book as a whole.

The "David and Goliath" story purely documents here an early understanding in history and that its message to us in the Second Millennium is still current: David was a little shepherd in the Kingdom of King Saul. One day shepherd David was called to play his harp in order to keep away the demons while the Philistines had declared war on the Kingdom under the powerful leadership of giant 'Goliath'.

When 'Goliath' met little 'David' he couldn't help but to burst out into laughter: "You better wear a war-kit instead of your ridiculous shepherd outfit." David responded to Goliath: "I put my trust into my God who will guide me." Goliath despicably pronounced that his many Gods were much more powerful than the only one of David." – "We will see about that!" Returned David and hurriedly pulled his slingshot towards Goliath scoring a fatal hit at his temple, which made Goliath fall dead to the ground. Thereafter David was declared a hero as the Philistines had lost their powerful leader. What has the quintessence become of it? Even a slingshot can make fall a giant.

Whether it is strength or health, everything again is relative as little causes often can lead to big effect, or by the saying of a proverb: Great oaks from little acorns grow. Strength and health inherent in us does not always become visible. We can build or neglect them of which the decision is left to us. From such deriving decisions a "Simple Life" can also become dependent.

CHAPTER 9

Being in Need of Help

Needing help in relation to acquiring a 'simple life' supports the adage, 'Where there is a will there is a way.' The fact that help is requested initiates a signal for others to join in the attempt to reach a goal through combined efforts. This however is only given when the party in need of help has personally established a base on which help can flourish. Crying for help while doing little or nothing oneself, can waste the time and efforts of those who have come to help.

What is understood about help with regard to reaching a 'simple life' and the signs that help is required? Actually, it is not much different from help for any other purpose! Firstly, it has to be reliably established who is worthy of help and who is not. A prerequisite here is a good relationship with other people as it is only human to stay away from those who exhibit arrogance and self-obsession.

Today, in a rapidly changing world, the lesser requirements of the 'needy' are easily overlooked. It is only through a conscious awareness of our fellow creatures that we are enabled to notice the needs of the genuinely disadvantaged. The process of recognising this is not entirely without risks. An apparent need usually is accompanied by an unknown background which, when disturbed by an outsider, can deter even the best of intentions.

Besides caution in dealing with issues of help, it is a requirement of the needy to seek openness out of a potentially reserved attitude. Here, the person in need has to actually signal for help before somebody can initiate lending a helping hand. Help offered to somebody in need is an essential part of a society's well-being. Without help available across all levels of society, there would only be a decrease in the numbers of those able to enjoy the 'simple life'. Fewer people would enjoy the so important personal freedom of choice. It is only from that standpoint that individuals can gain access to a 'simple life' within their own chosen societal group.

Unless unforeseen incidents such as dangerous situations prevail, words are usually the first contact with those in need of help. A good measure of adaptation, convincing attitudes and practical skills are then essential in winning the trust of the needy so that the help offered will convincingly assist towards a better life. This can happen only as long as initial words are translated into practical actions. Words alone have never changed much except perhaps by helping to bridge a situation momentarily or to put the lid on something to prevent it from boiling over. Words as well actions have to be tailored to the needs of the person who seeks help. It has never been ideal to impose one-sided conditions, because help can serve its purpose only when all parties become engaged in the same understanding. It needs the involvement of the helping hand as well as the receiving hand.

Help is also not meant to turn the one in need into a dependent. Rebuilding together that which has been lost is essential to attaining the stage where recovery can continue, independent of the one offering assistance. This of course requires a good deal of empathy, a mutual understanding and appropriate responses on both sides. It is also important that encouragement rather than just receipt of a benefit exists in situations of aid. If the short cut of just handing out a benefit is taken, the result will be continued dependence. This shifts the necessary goal of independence further out of reach. Therefore, it can be concluded that help, which does not support regaining comprehensive independence, should not be considered help at all.

Often, help is linked to conditions set by politically or privately motivated party interests, which can also lead to the wrong perception of help. This is especially true if there is not enough attention paid to the very personal needs of the party seeking help. If there is not enough circumspection in the whole help process, a lack of understanding and readiness for cooperation can result in hostile attitudes. This can barricade the person in need into a very tight position rather than setting them free.

Self-help is a desirable outcome for any kind of assistance. It eventually releases the helping hand to pursue other people in need of help. The idea of help is not that people get used to a helping hand, thus ceasing to contribute themselves. They should not fail to individually build on what has been received with the purpose of rebuilding missing parts in an incomplete life puzzle. Once such a 'puzzle' has been restored to a degree that a complete 'picture' remerges, minimum conditions have been met for a dignified human existence. Self-responsibility has to respond by continuing to build where the helping hand has handed over control i.e. when 'need' changes to 'want'. If such a process fails to materialise, help can institutionalise itself to the detriment of everybody involved. The 'needy' continue their dependency; the helping hand is locked into a narrow, individual life-circle and finally, others in the wider community are left to help from a distance.

It should be obvious that help is succeeding at its vocation only if the other side responds on equal terms. Recently, an author at a book talk happened to express the view that countries like the one he came from, South Africa, have very few extended social networks. Because of this, the people have much more supportive family lives because family members depend more on each other for help. A country with more complex social networks on the other hand, shows levels of dysfunction in an alarming number of families. Everybody considers themselves more individually secure and thus are less reluctant to care for the others.

This is a result of people having become accustomed to help from government organisations instead of assuming individual responsibility and contributing in return to the support system. What we have received in help, we should be obliged to return. This is a basic rule for a functional community life. Social or political critics do not welcome such a view today, as the 'people' would regard it in a highly negative fashion. Social welfare has become a measure of societal progress, overlooking some practical and non-practical measures of its own. When disconnected from de facto realities and ignored long enough, this type of support will reduce the entire social system to unwanted levels. We have only to continue long enough with social self-awareness and to wake up to its new realities.

Further details about social welfare are not needed as everybody who is aware enough can find proof of social miscarriage for him/herself. Clearly, this type of social system cannot deliver a 'simple life' for the majority. At best, a social system can support the individual in an underlying principle of personal freedom of choice, which moves that individual closer to a 'simple life'.

In addition to all the previously mentioned types who seek help, there is also the exemption to these stereotypes, the self-help individual. Again, quite a number of fundamentally different conditions play a role in such an individual's life. One might find this self-motivated person functioning at the bottom of the social scale. This then demands outstanding personal characteristics to move up that scale on his/her own. Here, success is an enduring achievement, seldom leaving behind marks of hardship, marks that can partly offset a desired goal. The individual who has seen better living conditions is the one who is more likely to succeed with self-help. This is because a comparison to his/

her actual situation can either stimulate an aspiration or lead towards indifference because of an inherent failure to act in time.

Self-help and help received from others warrants the question: who is in the majority, those needing help or those offering help? In order to deliver an answer, the attentive citizen should have experienced a need for help in his/her own life. Together with observing the lives of others this should indicate that we all, without exemption, need the help of others from time to time. It might just be help, combined with one's own efforts, with finalising the last part of a job when one's own will starts running out of steam. Without help, many goals could not be achieved. In our growing societies, teamwork has become a common password. In reality, this is nothing more than moving closer together and helping each other aspire to the best outcome.

All these issues surrounding the need of help on the way to the 'simple life' are best highlighted by a few examples from our incredibly colourful real world. In an allegory from the New Testament of the Bible, 'The Good Samaritan' shows how help can come from any number of people. In the times of early Christianity, help was held in high esteem among fellow humans. Jesus is said to have used the story to demonstrate to a scholar of law what a good person is like. In the parable, a merchant travelling from Jerusalem to Jericho is ambushed by a band of robbers, everything being forcibly taken away from him. Not even the merchant's own clothes are spared and he is badly beaten, leaving him helpless on the side of the road.

The first to come past the place is a priest who takes no notice of the merchant's dreadful situation. After a while, a number of high aristocrats also come past the critically injured merchant, also ignoring him because of the visible discomfort they experience from this sight. More time passes, leaving the merchant merciless and in the same dreadful situation on the side of the stony, dusty road exposed to the late afternoon heat.

Finally, a villager from Samaria, a Samaritan, comes to the place where the robbery has taken place. The Samaritan, unlike his predecessors, stops to check on the lonely creature in great need of help. Although not belonging to the richer upper class and not generally esteemed by society, he arduously carries the man from the side of the road to the next village, all on his own. The few dinars the Samaritan has with him he hands to a nursing home, together with the injured, helpless merchant so that they can take proper care of this person in urgent need of help.

It is not by accident that the so-called 'lower' ranked society members find time in the first place to care for others. The 'high' ranking society members on the other hand often are too busy just keeping their ranking in place. Only when reaching a point of compassion in a more independent move within a 'simple life', will more people, regardless of their status in society, rediscover help in order to serve the needy. The Samaritan ideology has survived in many forms today: the Red Cross, paramedics, ambulance services, first aid, and voluntary nursing of the elderly. Help is still recognised as a vital connecting link between our different societal ranks, because we all need it, eventually.

The relevance of the Good Samaritan analogy in today's society can be demonstrated by the almost daily occurrences of accidents. Unless a society's appointed organisation has been called to the scene of an accident, very little else is usually happening with regard to help. The 'priest' and 'high aristocrats' are still among us, mostly outnumbering the 'Samaritans'. The ones who have the means to help are most of the time too busy to have time available for unconditional help.

Sometimes reports circulate, telling us frankly how many people rushed past a particular accident before a 'Samaritan' found the courage to stop and find out what help is needed. Then later, we are all embarrassed because of having contravened our 'holy cow', the rule of helping others. Unfortunately, it remains a matter of fact that not many have the civil courage or drive to help effectively at the time it is most needed.

Another example from current times demonstrates this. Some equipment in a company catches fire because of an electrical fault. Smoke starts dropping in heavy clouds from the higher ceiling area. Everybody flees the area like frightened chooks, forgetting in their hurry that other people are left behind in the immediately affected area. There is however one man who makes the right decision. He rushes up the staircases armed with the appropriate fire extinguisher for electrical fires. Not only the equipment and the building are saved but also the lives of the people who in their confusion had run around like chooks without a head, not knowing what to do. The ratio of effective helpers to panic merchants would probably have amounted to fifty to one.

During a recent book launch by a South African author, the author noted that societies like South Africa have a poor welfare record within their social system. He did not criticise social progress outright but opened many eyes by establishing that personal relations within those societies of fewer welfare services are in better shape overall. This is because, particularly with families, everybody still depends on each other more.

Abandoning reciprocal responsibilities within a social environment can only be regarded as a flawed understanding of social progress. People often conclude that others are supported by a welfare system against the shortfalls of life. We should be able to recognise with unbiased, open views just how wrong this is. In order to help, one has to be constantly ready and not taking convenient breaks or holidays from caring for others in need of help. Education and the tradition behind it play their role in identifying a need for help, as the needy person is rarely the one who can or even wants to express the need for help. A fine line has also to be drawn between a real need for help and the abuse of proffered help. Only experiences gained in the real world can open a door towards an understanding of the need for help.

Further examples of help needed and help offered will show how today, a need for help affects everybody's daily life. Firstly, there are the more obvious situations that call for help.

How many times when keeping ourselves busy have we asked ourselves, "Why haven't I got a third hand"?

- On a builder's job site a helping hand can undoubtedly become useful when a lost nail for instance has to be recovered in order to continue. Who is going to search the ground for the nail or hand a replacement nail straight away?
- A pianist needs a sheet of music turned while both hands are busy with the keys. Here the third hand delivers the solution, too.
- A typist is interrupted by a phone call at the same time as a colleague asks for the phone book, which, in the rush, drops onto the floor. Again, two hands will not be enough to deliver immediate help.
- The bricklayer usually needs the extra workers to supply the mortar and the bricks to where the tradesman is busy raising a house wall - straight and plumb, brick by brick with one hand, and mortar off the trowel with the other hand. Here also an additional hand would be useful.
- In a train compartment, a suitcase is stored on a luggage rack above the seats. A woman wishes to get off the train at the next stop. Unable to reach the rack, she calls on the man opposite her who helped store it away initially. He lifts the woman's luggage off the rack but loses his grip. If the third person in the compartment had not quick-wittedly lent a hand to catch the case it would have fallen. Many hands helped safeguard a situation.
- During an operation, a surgeon certainly would not mind having even more than three hands for assistance, especially during complex procedures.
- A family member carries from the kitchen a tray with coffee mugs, plates, drinks, and food towards the house door leading

to the veranda. Without being specifically called upon to open and close the door, another family member hurries to help with that crucial third hand.

This list of innumerable daily occurrences could be extended; we all experience them every day if only we are mindful enough to notice. The extra helping hand always comes from fellow men and women. A connection to the 'simple life' is straightforward; a helping hand instantly can ease somebody else's burden, putting both the 'helping' and the 'receiving' hand on a path towards a 'simple life'.

Apart from these more obvious examples of help needed and given, there are also examples of less obvious ways help is needed. An individual's courtesy and awareness can help open avenues of assistance to those who are unaware of alternative ways to escape life's difficulties. Whether self-inflicted, inflicted from outside situations or just as a result of fate, the downside of life can appear insurmountable. Less obvious examples of help needed are found where people live. Neighbours, for instance, are never far from us but how much do we really know of each other? To draw out the idea further, friends and family are close to us and we should call for help here first before looking any further.

Help is always needed. However, it is not always obvious if we aren't caring compassionately for others. The busier we are ourselves, the less time is found to care for somebody or something else. Nevertheless, there is a fine line between self-care and care for others, as no real care or help can emerge without appropriate self-care happening first. The one who struggles with his/her individual situation can only become ready to help others when joint forces unite to help ease individual burdens in awareness for the other.

Helping one another builds friendships. How true is that? For a number of years Michael has been a close friend of Paul's, living across the road from each other. On hot summer days, they like to cool down in the town's public swimming pool. On weekends, especially when the two teenagers see each other, something in or around the house usually needs doing. Most of the time, one comes around to the other's place to lend a helping hand either with kitchen duties, cleaning the yard from fallen leaves, hosing and washing the family car or helping in the vegetable garden either with some weeding or watering. All those small duties can be done easier and quicker with a helping hand, which in return frees both Michael and Paul for leisure in the pool for a few hours of the afternoon. Help here is not a necessity but it contributes to a common cause within a friendship, which is a small step in the direction of a 'simple life'. More of this type of help can ease life's burden through friendly relations.

Help from friend to friend can be extended into families. Why shouldn't family relations include friendship? What makes a family strong is pulling the 'rope' of life in the one direction together and not in individually different directions. An 'old rule' still applies also to the family: 'If you want something, you have also to give something in return.'

The 'Holy Trinity' of politics is only bad news – 'I know something about you. I need something from you. I have something for you.' No relationship can last with such a focus on fellow humans because it is an invitation for corruption. Unconditional help that could be thought of as between friends should eventuate in an individual family as well as between the wider social family. On one side, it is commonly understood and seems to be so natural that a helping hand can do so much good to others. On the other side, reality stands in the way when the crucial step leading to positive action appears to be the difficult part. We always aim at securing our own interest first before either thinking or acting in a collaborative sense with fellow humans.

In that vein, neighbours should aim for friendly relations as well as those with families. Mostly we cannot choose our neighbours; therefore, it is good practice to maintain friendly relations with them if we are to value our own personal freedom. Again, an 'old rule' applies with neighbours: 'You are treated as you treat others.' A test of this rule can be seen in our daily interactions with our nearby neighbours. Nothing comes easy and this is particularly so as we strive for a better understanding with our neighbours. Even if in doubt about changing conditions within a neighbourhood, stronger maintenance of patience and adaptation will eventually help establish good neighbourhood relationships in the end.

This can be demonstrated when a next-door neighbour has gone away on a holiday. Instead of just cutting his own front lawn, a thoughtful neighbour cuts the lawn across both house fronts so that the whole frontage of the two properties looks neat. On returning from their holiday, the neighbours were very pleased to see that during their absence, their property had been looked after. This gave them relief from the quite natural worry when going away and leaving everything behind, even if for a limited time only. The following weekend the neighbour who had been away invited his 'good Samaritan' neighbour to a barbecue during which the latest news on the home front and that of the holiday were freely exchanged in a relaxed, friendly atmosphere. This was all due to that helping hand outstretched to cut the neighbour's lawn while they were away from home. Down to earth practical help is always the best way to keep up good relations with neighbours.

So far, help has focussed around customary life situations. What about 'help' though, that is outside the usual grind of daily life, obvious or not? A need for help will certainly not stop with just the close next-door neighbours. An entire street can benefit from good neighbourly relationships. An occupant's house should not have to catch fire to make their fellow citizens aware of help needed. The endless trivia of daily life makes up the vast majority of situations in which help is required. Assistance from outside can improve on other people's efforts and that quick spur of the moment help can further cement good relations.

For instance, a tree has fallen across a road during a late night storm. Traffic has come to a halt. A number of people turn away to take a side street while only a few of the passers-by help remove tree branches off a parked car to save it from further damage. This also gives everybody else a free passage after the damaged car has been removed. Common sense has to rule here in order to secure everybody's safety. Priority is given to the practical person who can discuss an action plan with everybody who wants to give a hand at the scene. A practical and secure joint effort can deliver the quick solution everybody wants.

A personal experience further demonstrates this point. While in Jundiai, Brazil, I saw a woman hit by a passing car as I came out of a shopping centre. She ended up in a terrible condition by the side of my parked car. Immediate help became a matter of urgency at that moment if she stood any chance of survival. Waiting for an ambulance was out of the question. A pedestrian actually took the first initiative, opening the sliding door on the side of my VW bus and without delay helped me put the woman on the back seat. Spontaneously, I asked the man to join me in the car on the direct way to the nearest hospital. The hospital staff acted immediately, as if having waited for this 'delivery'. They even asked us not to waste crucial moments and to carry the badly injured woman straight onto the operating table ourselves.

Afterwards, in an adjacent waiting room, a report over the accident had been documented from our statements. We were asked to wait for the first comments of the surgeon. When he came to see us, he said, "You were brave and quick; the woman would not have survived another minute on a transport. She might make it through now. I will let her know that your quick action saved her life and she can thank you herself. It is exceptional that people take action in such an urgent case in which a person's life is hanging on the thinnest possible thread." A few weeks later when I paid a visit to the hospital to find out how the woman had recovered, I was told that she had done well and had returned home. It came as no surprise that the woman never reconnected with her saviours. Humans are good at forgetting. However, taking 'positive' action in our lives remains one of the best things we can do.

Otherwise, we would succumb to the 'negative' aspects of life. Life, whether 'simple' or not, can flourish only in a positive, natural environment.

People in other parts of the world naturally live in different conditions from those to which we have become accustomed. Observant onlookers will recognise in particular that a great number of countries still present a mixed image of living standards in which poverty's presence cannot be missed. The sheer number of people in the world that still live in poverty in the 21st century raises many questions for those who are conscious of their fellow humans beings' living conditions. It is not as simple as asking a single question about how poverty came to be so widespread, and it is difficult for the outsider to recognise variations in poverty simply by meeting people.

At first glance, the observer from a very different societal background might think all poor people look the same. However, real help for the genuinely needy requires empathy as well as insight. It is vital not to meddle improperly into individual concerns and social mores. In a confrontation with poverty, the ones in need of help have to be convinced of aid which he/she can understand so that the all important mutual trust can develop. Somebody in tatters on the side of a dusty road looks at the world around him very differently from that of an incidental 'ring-in'. We can ignore this other side because of a conviction that this is not 'my fault' and continue with a life of 'miserable comfort'. Alternatively we can care about others and help by interceding in order to show a light at the end of the tunnel of poverty. Then we can all move towards a more decent 'simple life'.

As well as the obvious and the not so obvious need for help in society, there are also situations in which the need for help is provoked. You call the 'shots' but also you have to accept the unforeseen circumstances in which others are asked to help rescue what didn't go to plan. This is what 'provoked help' is all about. Some examples should facilitate an understanding of how diverse 'simple life' issues are and how paths can lead towards or away from them.

Most people enjoy watching racing cars in action as they roar at high speed, driven by others around a set circuit. As long as everything goes to plan, nobody worries much. However, inevitably the driver is confronted with a situation he cannot entirely control any more. The excitement, together with the raised blood pressure of the spectators, contributes to a driver's exertion. He may be winning, falling behind, losing or displaying a spectacular accident in which a stand-by team is asked to pick up the pieces and see how a puzzle might come together again. Help in those cases has been 'provoked' because of the risks known from the start but ignored for the sake of a goal that is set above the potential for disaster.

Most of the time it is money driving this kind of risk-taking. In the case of a race to inspire confidence, all sorts of side efforts come to the party in order to play down the danger role. The one who starts a race always needs to know what the stakes are: glory and money for a winner, often nothing or very little for the losers and a degree of trouble for the one who ends up in an accident. Spectators, on the other hand, are drawn by chance, keeping their fingers crossed for their hero. Such a diversion of outcomes causes a gambling situation for everybody, the race driver, the race team and the dedicated spectators. The real issues of technology and the money behind it put everybody into a position of high expectations. Under such varying conditions, help is a far cry away from any 'simple life'.

Even the winner is under renewed pressure to repeat a performance, which only raises the stakes of another win versus a failure. The ones behind the scene that actually benefit from their set goals are at best exchanging the difficulties and challenges others carry with a much simpler life. Help has become here only a piece in a puzzle that fits a bigger picture drawn by others. Of course, the spectacle of a race is always bait and when the stakes are high enough, can guarantee the best excitement, but not necessarily the best outcome.

Greyhounds can show us a bit about the nature of races. Their hungry, 'skin and bones' look adds to the excitement. The dogs race after the bait while organisers and spectators sit in relative comfort spinning their yarns and gambling for the best odds. All nerves are on 'tenterhooks', raising daily stress levels to new heights by leaving everything else behind for a limited time. However, the awakening in the race's aftermath can easily raise stress levels even higher, depending on whether there has been a win or a loss. A race is a walk on the edge towards a 'simple life'.

A climber on a mountain, alone or in a team is regarded as courageous at least as long as everything goes to plan. As soon as the climber's abilities become overstretched, it is danger time, which calls upon others to step in with help in order to rescue their fellow humans, their plans, and often their materials too. In the case of a rescue mission, it should never be forgotten that rescuers have to face the same hurdles undertaken by the daring adventurer. There is a fine line between managing a challenge responsibly and a carefree attitude of 'come what may, somehow it will work out'.

Man is known for his inquisitiveness, a liking for pushing the existing boundaries further and further. The result is often that others are called upon to follow, usually in more cautious footsteps, to save a mission undertaken in the name of progress. We have certainly become used to a life with progress and do not want to miss out. Nevertheless, progress for the climber too has at least its two sides: one step forward, one step backwards depending each time on which one surpasses the other. A larger backwards step provokes the need for help whereas the one forward can be assisted with help. We all have heard also about costly rescue missions with regard to humans and materials.

Where is the link to a 'simple life' in these situations? Any kind of help can ease a situation with the difference however of whether the 'direct road' is taken or the 'roundabout way' is taken. A win or an achievement on the 'direct road' is born out of courage and has its justification as long as difficulties have been left behind. On the other hand, failure to master a challenge introduces setbacks, not any more on one's own accord but forced on to others, still leaving the options open towards a 'simple life'. The nature of help, whether obvious, non-obvious, or provoked are vital signs on the road to a 'simple life'.

CHAPTER 10

Staying Honest or Grappling with Dishonesty

Quite a number of arguments arise around the question of whether or not honesty has become an exhibition piece in a museum and not commonly found in society anymore. Again, the main thing is that everybody has heard of it but most conveniently leave it for others to practise.

What is honesty and does it pay to adhere to staying honest? Honesty is something we can neither see, measure nor physically grasp. So how can we relate to it then? By studying its opposite, dishonesty, we can quickly become aware of the meaning of honesty. When trust becomes part of our dealings with other people, a failure to respect this trust will enlighten either party to the difference between honesty and dishonesty. It is usually expectations that foster trust and when they cannot be met, mistrust often introduces dishonest dealings as a consequence.

Many illustrations exemplify the dichotomy of honesty and dishonesty. When buying something, prior information has usually prepared us for the product we seek. A car dealer's self-perception will convince him that he never tries to sell a 'bad product'. It has to be good no matter what the circumstances are. Everything then becomes 'base flattery', targeting the customer's trust and the inspection of his wallet. Product options range in most cases from the very basic to the luxury model.

Here, customer satisfaction is a highly desirable outcome, especially for the customer, as he/she is the one who wants the best deal for what is on offer. On the other hand, the car dealer is competing with customer interest for another benefit, one of his own. When both interests, dealer's and customer's, meet on common ground, neither party feels belittled. For that moment at least, the parties can be considered honest.

The more often this common ground is shifted apart e.g. when the dealer arguments are stronger than customer expectations, the more often customer dissatisfaction is likely to surface. Usually these 'wake up calls' occur mainly on the customer's part. However, flexibility in adjusting an unexpected outcome in the deal can keep both parties honest.

Only major satisfaction on both sides indicates honest dealings between people while one-sided satisfaction in an outcome usually indicates dishonest dealings. Dissatisfaction will not go away on its own, haunting one side often in unwanted and unexpected ways, a backlash that lingers on.

Staying honest has a close relationship to helping others. A real desire to help, no matter what the occasion might be, is born out of honesty from a direct response to benefiting somebody else in achieving a simpler outcome. The general masses largely keep the key to simplicity or to difficulty in life. Out of this desire to help comes the adage, 'You are treated as you treat others'.

The 'recipe' for all this sounds quite simple but it still needs circumspection in different situations. Out in the 'real world' more negative interactions than we would like are found. Fraudsters do not treat the other side equally, no matter how they have been treated. Self-interest is their motto. Beware of these people! Honesty and its divergences of dishonesty, trickery, and imposture are not only present when dealing with objects; we successfully play those questionable games in interpersonal relationships too. Here, honesty can have a big impact on an individual's wellbeing, depending on which side we embark.

Friends and families rely on, and relate to, each other mainly by staying honest. Where there is no honesty, no relationship can be born. We all need that assurance from others on which we can build our lives together. Uncertainties in relationships brought about by doubts in honesty, delay the individual's efforts in moving towards the very distant 'simple life'. Honesty is further sought from the very beginning of human relationships, friendship and family. The less a direct relationship can be relied on (because more self-interest enters the equation) the more dependent people become on the social welfare system. We have to recognise the differences in dealing with a close friendship, a family, a business or politics.

The same platitudes can have different meanings on the different social levels as interests play their role. A good politician for instance has always looked at people's mouths, using platitudes or commonplace expressions in order to be heard in the first place. After a connection has been established between the constituency of a politician for instance, everything else from then on is left to interpretation. It is here where honesty can lose ground with individuals when interests highjack their mandate.

This sort of deviation from what we want and can expect in a power game is an almost daily reality. However, if this digression gets a firm footing in our friendships and families, it most certainly will corrupt everything else. In that case, honesty has gone missing from the start and cannot add further positive outcomes into the wider community. Results then will almost certainly be mistrust, feeding on failed expectations. Therefore, it is of a significant importance that the healthy status of honesty be the basis in friendships and families. Problems that start on early levels only grow within a wider community, ultimately calling into question a society's function. In addition, everything starts small even the many building blocks of honesty.

In the past, tradition has laid the foundations, positive or not, for an upcoming generation to continue. The Second Millennium seems to question everything that link individuals with societies. However, it remains to work out where all this is supposed to lead. Experience from the past should indicate that rarely does something turn out better after abandonment of, for instance, the belief in a system of honour and honesty. It is better to engage in a cautious step-by-step continuity.

As early as 570 BC, the Greek poet Aesop demonstrated a lesson in his fable, 'The Woodman and the Axe'. This lesson was the age-old one of 'Honesty is the best policy'. In the fable, it is said that a woodcutter worked on the banks of a river beside where the forest closed in. While swinging his axe, he lost his firm grip on the handle and could only watch as the axe disappeared into the rushing water of the river next to him.

What could the woodcutter do? Inconsolable, he sat next to the river wishing he had his axe back, while his eyes filled with tears. The god Mercury heard this sorrowful lament and immediately came to the rescue of the woodman. In front of the surprised woodman, Mercury dived into the river and retrieved a golden, shiny axe from the river depths. Showing it to the woodman, he asked him, "Is this your axe?" The woodman denied ownership of the beautiful and expensive golden axe. Mercury returned to the river, this time bringing out a shiny silver axe. Again, the woodman told Mercury that this axe also was not his. Surprised by this honest man, Mercury finally removed from the river the steel axe that the woodman had lost. "Is this your axe?" "Yes indeed, thank you so much," responded the woodman. Mercury then rewarded the honest woodman by giving him the silver and golden axes as well as his original steel one.

On returning to his home, the excited woodman told his family and friends about his lucky experience. Without telling anybody, a friend who heard the woodman's story, took himself to the same river. He also took an ordinary steel axe and after throwing it into the river stood lamenting on the riverbank. Mercury heard his plea and diving into the river pulled out a golden axe. However, when the question was asked, "Is this your axe?" the answer from the man was, "Yes, this is my axe." Mercury was not prepared to honour this twisting of an honest man's story into one of self-interest. In an instant, the golden axe was returned to the river to join the steel axe on the riverbed. Mercury disappeared as suddenly as he had appeared, leaving the dishonest man high and dry without any axe.

Honesty, as in this fable, also serves to educate people on how to move closer towards experiencing a 'simple life'. Avoiding an honest life can cause unnecessary difficulties. However, in the real world there is always 'wants' lined up against established 'power'. The choice remains with the individual. Will one bank more on personal freedom through honesty or take chances away from it to travel down the road of dishonesty. In addition, before saying to our children that 'Honesty is the best policy', shouldn't we seriously embark on making the world an honest place. In other words, do not expect others to lead the charge on making an honest world; this alone cannot be turned into reality. Reality is always there and has to be respected, often contravening individual aspirations. Staying honest sometimes appears to be a call only to the less 'important' man so that the fewer 'smart' people can navigate around it for the sake of self-interest.

A modern day example points towards the same conclusion i.e. staying honest ensures people are socially better off within a community. This is because everything is done and said directly, with a focus on simplicity, instead of in difficult and roundabout ways. An everyday occurrence from two different viewpoints shows this:

Michael is in town doing the usual weekly shopping in the town's main shopping complex. He uses his car to transport the goods home, which is a few kilometres too far to tackle on foot. At the cashier, he suddenly becomes aware that he can't find his wallet in the back pocket of his jeans. His immediate thoughts were, "Did I leave it at home, leave it in the car or lose it on the way in on foot?" Anyway, he had to leave the goods in the shop and go investigating the loss of his wallet.

Back at his parked car, Michael turned everything upside down in the car with no results. Driving home afterwards to search his house likewise did not deliver the wallet with the money for the shopping. He began to think that maybe a pickpocket had pinched it in the shopping area or that possibly he had lost it and an honest person had handed it into the lost property office. Despite not believing in this last option, the best Michael could do was to go back to the shopping centre and find out for himself. Following the exact same path from the car park didn't reveal any trace of the wallet. Finally, Michael paid a visit to the lost property office.

After having given his personal details, the man at the counter smiled and turned towards the back of the office. When he returned, Michael could not believe his eyes. There was his wallet in the man's hand. "Only an hour ago, a young bloke turned this wallet in. I can give you his name and address. If this is your wallet, tell me what is in it." Surprisingly, nothing was missing. The wallet was found in the car park area and the honest young man turned it into the office. While getting out of the car, the wallet must have been pushed up and out of Michael's back pocket, dropping unnoticed on the ground next to the car.

Even before returning to the food store, Michael went to the address, rewarding the finder with an appropriate monetary reward. At first, the finder refused to accept the reward but gave in at the insistence of Michael after both realised that they were basketball players at the same club, just in different divisions. Honesty in returning the wallet not only rewarded both but also started a new friendship through their sports connection.

How might the situation possibly have turned out if the finder had kept the lost wallet? Firstly, Michael would have been very sad, acknowledging the loss of his wallet with all its contents. What about the dishonest finder? Could he really become a 'lucky' person? The money from the wallet allowed the finder to satisfy several dreams, which he could not wait to do.

Out went the money from the wallet, paying for a luxury DVD player in one of the electronic shops at the shopping centre. As a precaution, the wallet itself ended up in a rubbish bin. This 'proud owner' took the goods to his car, deciding to look for his friends to show them what he had bought. While he returned in a hurry to the shopping centre, he didn't realise that somebody else had watched him with the new, luxury DVD player. The DVD player and his own negligently discarded wallet on the passenger seat drew the attention of car thieves. In no time, they found their way into the car, neither removing the DVD player nor the obviously visible wallet, but taking everything away with the car.

Returning from the shopping centre with two of his friends, the man could not believe the loss of his car. This crook had found his master, learning a lesson that in the world of dishonest people nothing stops others from taking somebody else for a ride. He who harms others is likely to be harmed himself. The seed one sows is the crop one can expect. Sowing honesty will become a crop of a 'simple life' too.

CHAPTER 11

Ignoring or Respecting our Fellow Creatures

What is the meaning of 'respect'? This word originates from the Latin *re*, which means 'back', while 'spect' derives from *specere* meaning 'to look at'. Hence, 'respect' means 'to look back at'. 'To look back at' is an invitation to look, not just forwards into a wishful future, but also to consider where something originates from, including man himself. Comprehension of the past enables us to move forward uninterrupted into both the near and the distant future.

With regard to our fellow human beings, respect simply means stopping the usual drive for more, quicker or better things in our lives, in exchange for listening to what somebody else has to say. If we choose the self-interest pathway, it might temporarily lead to success more quickly but an African proverb shows the downfall of this way. 'If you want to go **fast**, you have to go it alone; but if you want to go **far,** you have to go it together'. These are choices in life and we know quite well how to distinguish between a single 'performer' and others who join in and share both the challenges as well as the achievements.

One difference however is that the single performer is less likely to be on good terms with or to respect his fellow creatures as his 'single lane move' doesn't allow much circumspection. All his/her efforts are directed towards future obstacles with little or no regard for followers, let alone 'overtakers'. Such a 'single lane' position inevitably leads to isolation whereas team operators establish 'multiple lanes' from the start. This gives options for advancement to more people, allowing also caution for respect and other important aspects of life.

A few practical examples will highlight the results of integrating 'respect' into a life that can move towards being a 'simple life'. The majority of people acknowledge verbally that 'respect' is one of the best-regarded virtues, while in daily life we still forget to practise it to this level. Real 'respect' is only exemplified in actions and doesn't need much of a 'talk fest'. Instead, an exemplar action is, and always will be, the best teacher. If we complain about 'respect' it mainly shows the lack of teaching by example.

The following examples of situations dealing with 'respect' should stimulate discussion on how they knowingly, as well as innocently or naively, affect life. It is interesting to note too that it is only humans who have a problem with 'respect'. All other life forms have their lives regulated by what we call 'instincts', which so far has protected them in their fight for survival. In nature, the elderly are considered wiser and more experienced, which results in wiser behaviours from which the young learn. These behaviours are then integrated into the lives of the younger animals. A young dog for instance, respects the older dog without question, begging for approval in his unstoppable drive to survive. A warning growl stops the young dog's liberal attempts. Licking the older dog's lips rearranges the 'respect order' between the young underdog and the superior age and experience of the older dog.

Humans on the other hand don't have that straightforward way of passing on 'respect'. Challenging 'respect' has instead almost become an intellectual movement in our understanding. However, it is exactly because of intellect's involvement that we have shortcomings in controlling our actions as the intellect is 'roaming' without limitations. A lack of 'respect' can also be a result of ignorance. Our experience with respect is certainly different from that of the aforementioned dogs. We can study the innumerable examples of respect being ignored or respect being paid between our fellow creatures.

(a) Ignoring respect

> A train station at peak traffic time sees a great number of people rushing in and out from constantly arriving and departing trains. Almost everybody is in a hurry to get through the doors of each compartment as quickly as possible. One door however allows only one person at a time to pass through. Depending on a person's readiness to push through the door, movement can sometimes be faster or can momentarily slow.
>
> A woman with a suitcase tries to move with the queue in her compartment's corridor towards the door, failing however to progress as the majority of passengers successfully push past her to get through the door onto the platform. The woman starts getting worried and insecure about whether she will make it out of the train during the stoppage time. 'First come, first succeeds' appears to be the governing rule, leaving the less pushy people stranded. The alternate option would be that some people within the crowd would look back and encourage the slower ones to move along with the queue. The message is simple: everybody takes that bit more time to allow others to catch up with the general flow.
>
> The pressure doesn't end however at the train's door. The next problem for the woman waits at the entrance into the main hall of the railway station. At the end of a tunnel passage under the railway lines, a swing door leads into the large station hall. Everybody going that way has to use this door. The quicker passengers take

their chance, squeezing through the door's opening before it swings back into the closed position. The woman with the suitcase however doesn't make the passage before the door swings back from a previous passenger, slamming hard into her suitcase. Luckily, she was carrying her case in front of her; otherwise, the door could have hit her right in the face.

People emerging from behind put their hands on the door in order to open the passage again mainly for themselves. During this move the woman too manages her passage through the door, leaving her wondering about people's rush to push their way blindly through the door without sparing a moment to 'look back' at others' attempts. Everybody could have achieved his or her goal in a much more respectful manner. The second somebody wants to be ahead of the others, respect for those others diminishes. One solution would be that everybody could organise their daily timetable better, allowing time to spare so that other people's needs might also be met. No matter how busy we feel, we should never forget that we are not alone in the everyday rush.

In races, we establish rules, one of which ought to be respect for other 'competitors' as a matter of course. When rules are broken in said races, the most likely consequences will be real damage or accidents. This won't be much different from the respect 'rule' even if the fallout is not always directly harmful or visible at once. It is however the little things in life which essentially help our bigger endeavours to get off the ground. The degree to which we can help ease the burdens of others through 'looking back' helps us gain our own goal of moving forward with their support in return.

The world has been and still is full of surprises. Some people may experience more of it than others. The woman with the suitcase couldn't stop another incident catching her by surprise. On leaving the station hall, down a flight of stairs leading to the footpath, a young skateboarder shoots past, barely missing her. The woman instantly loses her grip of the suitcase. "Not so fast young man; I'm also here," the woman reminds the lad. The skateboarding pedestrian again was somebody in a hurry with his vision focussed too far ahead. He wanted to get himself far away quickly and was not so much concerned with anybody else's needs. Conflict with regard to the 'rules' of respect led here to harming somebody else instead of helping to ease an individual situation through working together with our fellow creatures.

As our fate is usually destined, one mishap seldom arrives alone. The woman with the suitcase encountered another incident on the tram on her way home. Peak hour traffic was everywhere and many other people wanted to board the tram, which stopped only a short distance from the station. This time however, a man assists the woman by carrying the suitcase up the steep steps and into the tram. While the woman watches from the platform, the automated doors start to close, leaving her behind. The helpful man noted the situation however and quickly informed the tram driver, requesting he stop again to allow the woman to join her suitcase in the tram. "You are a true gentleman for not leaving me behind. Thank you so much," responds the woman appreciatively.

As the tram picks up speed, the woman can hardly keep her balance between the rows of passengers, bumping against everybody else who stands next to her. The crowd at least prevents her from falling over. Meanwhile, those in the occupied seats around her can't seem to see who is more in need of a seat. Nobody speaks a word. Everybody seems to be preoccupied with keeping their place in the tram by avoiding looking at each other, especially those standing. The ticket 'rule' satisfies the majority of people that they have the right to occupy a seat in the first place. It is only if none is available that they have to put up with standing. Again, first come; first served.

The strong young man in the seat next to the standing woman could well and truly make use of his youth and strength to take a standing position in exchange for forfeiting his seat for the suitcase woman. As long as nobody argues this point, let alone moves to initiate it, everything remains as it is. If we could read the minds of the people around the suitcase woman and that of the woman herself, it would demonstrate that they all have a conscience about the situation but their inner 'filthy swine' overcomes them as they hide from the less pleasant realities. Here it would have meant exchanging a comfortable seat with somebody else who is more in need and perhaps even exchanging compliments for mutual pleasure.

What could people have on their minds in a crowded tram regarding the ignoring or paying of respect? It very much depends on the timing. During workdays, people are more commonly preoccupied with business. In the morning, it can be a focus on possible future events, while at the end of the day the focus shifts away from daily business onto events of a private nature and a recovery from daily toil with an attempt at relaxation.

The person trying to catch up with relaxation while on the tram is probably happy enough to occupy a seat and is little concerned about other people's comfort. "I'm alright; that's what I pay for - to travel on the tram." The one who is closely cramped, standing in the passageway of the tram keeps a certain displeasure to himself. "What can I do; tomorrow might be a better day." Occasionally these people voice their anger with others by pushing for comfort that is more personal. They try to claim a seat, which will be theirs regardless of anybody else. A business battle is then extended even onto the tram. 'First come, first served' is their parole. However, there is still the patiently standing passenger, quietly reading a book, which can help divert the mind in order to ease the discomfort of standing.

The suitcase woman is probably clinging to the fact that at least somebody helped her to get on the tram. She wonders to herself, "What have so many people to do that they choose to take no action? They cannot all come from one and the same place and be going where I'm going. The good-looking, strong man on the seat next to me should be able to keep his balance better than I can do when standing. This however is nothing new. In today's world, more people are in a hurry than is good for them. They probably are not even aware any more that everything they do is one big rush. And for what purpose? I've seen worse; this is not the end of my world. At home at least, a nice cup of tea is waiting for me, which helps wash away the unpleasant moments of the day."

When the ticket man makes his presence felt on the tram, there could be unexpected movement in the crowd. A few are suddenly in a hurry to get out, leaving others to take their chances and push their luck for a seat. The suitcase woman still could not make it to a seat because the determination of others won over the discretion to help the needy. Despite a sign inviting passengers to be courteous and provide seating for the needy, such a request gets too easily overlooked in the rush. What remains remarkable however is that on the surface most people 'hide' quietly in their seats whereas their minds would tell very different stories, reflecting on the colourful palette of individual characters.

Everybody here at least pretends to know about the fine details of mutual respect. However, they take up a silent position, giving everybody else priority to come forward first. Regarding respect, this could be called a lack of civil courage, an uncertainty-driven self-protection: don't burn your fingers! The shortage of people coming forward out of natural respect also draws attention to the many women or men who seem to have parted ways with respect. Respect spans all activities in human relationships and is more of a silent companion today. However, it is still important to ease relations by calling attention to other people's concern and well-being in a close neighbourhood.

(b) Flight from respect

Out of insecurity and fear, certain people can take flight when getting involved in, or even causing, an accident. This is a lack of respect towards fellow creatures at its worst. Having failed in respecting a set of traffic lights for instance, an accident occurs. It doesn't make it better by fleeing the scene instead of staying to assist in limiting the damage, especially for the other party.

Spitting on a footpath is not much different from a dog leaving its mark behind. People have sensitivities around which rules have been established in order to secure standards on which the majority agree. Respect here can be seen as a natural superstructure regulating very basic inter-human relations. When challenging common rules of respect, it can only make sense to the extent that a countermeasure can successfully stand up. Otherwise, brutalisation becomes dominant over everything else we cherish. In the smallest 'bud', the underlying principles for future developments can be seen. Therefore, it is in the small details of respect rules that one can find the key for good relations with our fellow creatures. Relationship quality as a road sign to a 'simple life' depends to a degree on realisation: realisation that whoever best reads such signs and converts them into practice can count on a 'simple life'.

An example of bad practice is calling somebody abusive nicknames or swearing at them, which likewise shows a lack of respect towards one's fellow creatures. In that case, one can only expect to be treated the same way one has treated others. So when dealing with others roughly, one cannot expect to be treated with kid gloves. It is in our actions and expressions that we overlook possible outcomes by evoking, 'the means will justify the end', which in turn ensures the unpredictability of future outcomes. The only exemption would be that a joke is delivered this way: in that case however, the parties exchanging nicknames and swear words, need to be on friendly terms, knowing each other quite well so that there is no misunderstanding. In any case, to ignore respect is like walking on a knife's edge, not knowing to which side the initiative might turn - acceptance, confirmation or rejection from the opposite side.

On certain hours during the week, a town's centre becomes crowded with mainly local people. Neighbours, friends, relatives, acquaintances, and work colleagues can all bump into each other, expecting at least the usual 'hello'. Failure to get that simple courtesy registers mostly a negative reaction and provokes a plethora of negative feelings: "Why the hell is he ignoring me?" or "What is so bad he couldn't manage a simple friendly 'hello'?" or "Since when are we strangers with each other?" or "I can't believe that he missed seeing me." or "The bastard has his five minutes again." or "Does he reckon he is something better?" or "Maybe he didn't see the forest for the trees." or "The poor bugger must be worrying himself grey." Everything then becomes possible in one's mind simply because that courteous little word 'hello', was missing. Instead of a 'simple life', all these imaginings can come between our fellow humans and us.

What does life look like when respect is duly paid? It is simple. If one makes that first move towards expressing 'respect', the other side is won over already without waiting for a response. Perhaps the other person will come forward with a gesture of respect but this can never be taken for granted. This therefore allows uncertainty to establish itself in human relations.

The most basic and easiest respect rule of saying 'hello' or 'good day' to somebody else can lead to many reactions. We have all experienced the situation where even somebody we couldn't relate to instantly pays attention to us with a 'good day'. What this is doing is pulling us out of lethargy straight into alertness, starting with surprise and followed by our own cautious, respectful response. After such an encounter, we often continue thinking, "Since when did that person know me?" Regardless of the answer, a friendly, positive attention has introduced people to each other in a simple and straightforward way. Even the naturally reserved person then wakes up to the invitation of exchanging respect. It is not common but does happen occasionally that we come across a menacing looking person who seems to reject any respect offered. Eventually though, one can enhance the experience by overcoming the uncertainty with friendly respect. Sometimes that is all a situation needs to overcome a person's questionable reservation.

Much less attention is needed when meeting already established acquaintances. That initial hesitation is not present. We can therefore relate directly to the other person so that a wider exchange can take place. This can happen either with common knowledge or with new knowledge to be exchanged. Above all though, it must be under the custody of paying due respect. Exchanges can be direct, giving the benefit of an easier understanding. However, because of a closer intimacy, these exchanges can sometimes backfire into open hostility if both sides cannot primarily exchange kindness based on mutual respect.

Despite acquaintances' intimate knowledge of each other, respect can sometimes lead to misunderstanding, which again defeats the purpose of respect. "Hi lazy fellow; what are you doing in town during a working day? Don't tell me you are busy; the weather is too nice for that. I know what to expect from your lot." Such a form of address can, by a hair's breadth, turn the scale into either a convenient joke or an inconvenient embarrassment. Respect has therefore, to be above all, worthy of credit in order to not unwittingly unleash misunderstandings, the most common source of interpersonal relationship failure.

Some religious cultures, especially Buddhism, advocate respect on all occasions and to all life forms in a firm tradition, which not every religion can claim. The devoted sign of respect in Buddhist culture is demonstrated by placing both hands, palms together and pointing to the front, along with a nod of the head towards the other person in a gesture of affirmation. This takes place on either side, guest or host. Such a mutual devotion renders everybody equal in contrast to the subservient gestures of respect more commonly found in other cultures or religious traditions. Respect exchanged in an equally accepted formality has the merit of people meeting on equal terms and subordinates differences, at least for moments.

Like everything else, respect lives with us in practical terms. It is little use if well-hidden in mere lip service instead of showing it every day. What cannot be practised is rather worthless. There are so many occasions to come forward with a gesture of respect that we have only to seize on the opportunities. Like everything else, after having left the failures behind the truth is that enjoyment comes with continuous practise of being respectful. These are good lessons if we can learn from them.

However, one disappointment or failure alone will not be the end of the world. A young man dressed up in his special glad rags waits for his girlfriend so they can go to the cinema together. On this occasion, he wanted to invite her to dinner afterwards so that they could enjoy the rest of the day together. To give the occasion a special touch, the young man thought of buying a small bunch of red carnations, which he held in one of his hands while waiting patiently. After the meeting time had come and gone, the young man's patience was put to the test when the girlfriend had not turned up. His thoughts bounced from disapproval to apprehension. However finally he takes matters into his own hands, returns home, jumps into his car, and sets out to find out what is going on.

At the house of the girlfriend, nobody answers his call. "What the hell is going on? Has she forgotten about our meeting?" Luckily, the technology of the mobile phone delivers the answer soon after. Both the young man and his girlfriend were waiting in different places convinced that they were both right. Doubts immediately gave way to joy on both sides despite the cinema visit having been missed. Instead, the flowers spoke a language free of misunderstandings when the pair finally met in the place where the girl was waiting.

The original idea of a late Saturday afternoon trip to the cinema followed by a restaurant visit was thwarted. Instead, it turned into an excursion on foot into the beautiful, naturally established City Botanical Gardens. The bunch of flowers rivalled the garden's flowers and shone magnificently in the late afternoon sunshine. There was time to talk, relax and enjoy each others' company. This alternative proved a much better outing of their own rather than in the cinema crowd and restaurant world with its rather expensive food and drinks. There was nothing more to worry about as the respectful gesture of the floral offering had opened the door to a much simpler but more meaningful enjoyment.

Respect can also be seen in different actions throughout history. Early civilizations produced individuals who performed outstanding acts of kindness and respect in their time. A victorious warrior, for instance, often laid his claim to a position of leadership, introducing his own rules, which helped him to his victory. Rules were then demanded and enforced, and subjects were asked to show respect for the rules.

During the course of history, tradition has generally assured that a succession of descendents enjoy the right of rule. With this rule should have come respect even though the qualities of the originator were not met anymore. In the course of such degenerative behaviour, rules of respect developed in different directions within the growing societies. In order to meet more of the requirements of today's mega-societies, rules were established that allow societies still to function despite a shrinking individual base from which to operate.

In the past, a constant fine-tuning of existing respect has taken place. However, in recent times, calling said rules into question has become the mark of our time. Increases in crime, hooliganism, bullying at school, divorces in families, and breakdowns in friendships are the alarming signs of a move away from respectful behaviours. Each generation has to make its own effort to identify itself with the past while accommodating the present. It is not good enough just to take over from somebody else or to abandon what the ancestors have cherished.

Changes that incorporate the past also ensure rules of respect are not abandoned which would then lead to the inevitable consequence of increased friction in societal relations. To avoid such complications in life, we need to remember that everything starts off small. Moreover, we have to stay circumspect, alert enough to nip any difficulties in the bud before they grow into a difficult to control problem. This maintenance of respect has always been a helpful partner in the search for a 'simple life'.

Family respect can be highlighted by this Finnish fairytale (Z. Topelius 1818-1898). A family with a lot of little children lived a fairly deprived life in a small country town. The grandfather shared his life with them under the same roof. Because of his age, he was very weak and couldn't eat independently when at the family table. Holding the spoon alone became a struggle for him, which upset the parents who told the grandfather, "We've enough trouble teaching the children to eat on their own and don't need the same trouble on top of that with you. When you can't manage to eat anymore on your own, it's better that you stay in the corner room of the house with the pigs and share food with them." The grandfather naturally became so upset, questioning the parents, "Where are the help and the respect which I gave you in your lives?" He couldn't however reverse their lack of respect for he was too frail.

One son felt compassion for the grandfather, paying him a visit every so often even if it was just for a short time. After a while, an idea occurred to him. Unnoticed, he started working a piece of a tree stump with a woodcarving knife. When the parents became aware of it, they questioned the son, "What are you doing and what is it good for? You shouldn't work with dangerous tools like that." The son told the surprised parents, "I'm working on your trough so that when you get old, you can join the pigs and have your meals out of this trough in the company of the pigs." This made the parents think about the lack of respect they had paid the grandfather. Ashamed not only of their humiliating action but also of their way of thinking, they instantly changed their lack of respect for the grandfather into due respect. From then on, as is right and proper, the grandfather received the assistance of every family member to stay at the table for dinner. Sometimes it is just a matter of awareness that can move people's attitude of 'ignoring respect' to one of 'duly paying it to fellow creatures'. The Bible's 'Ten Commandments' express this in the fourth commandment: Respect your father and mother so that you also can live a long and fulfilling life on earth.

CHAPTER 12

Embarking on the Righteous Side of Life

'Embark' has the connotation of boats on water. Life can be compared to an ocean that carries all the individual human 'boats'. The ocean is a truly alive element, which can change in an unpredictable way from calm to wildly rough, leaving boats with little choice but to follow and battle the elements for survival. The ones surviving relatively unharmed in that ocean prove to themselves and to everybody else that they have chosen the righteous side of their lives. Obviously, an abundance of problems seems to be the opposite of it. Is that really the case? Don't we all go through phases of difficulties in our lives? It is not a given matter of fact that the calmer ocean will automatically be reached. It is only by surmounting problems that a calmer ocean can be discovered.

A survey of this topic begs the question, "What does 'the righteous side of life' really mean?" To understand the meaning of 'righteous' we need to understand its opposite, 'wrongful'. It has always been known that the right way has always been the shortest one to get us to where we want to go. And who really wants to intentionally go on long roundabout ways in life? Therefore, it can also be regarded as practical to stay on the 'righteous side of life'.

Looking a bit more realistically at this topic, 'righteous' could be reckoned as being only common sense which we all claim to have more or less already inherited. Now let us get more realistic and look at what it can reveal to us. 'Righteousness' has the power to stand on its own but it is often accompanied by the virtues 'honesty', 'directness', 'promptness', 'reliability', 'perseverance', 'trust', 'courage' and 'consideration'; altogether they form the stronger sides of life.

This Hans Christian Andersen fairy tale, "What the father does is always righteous," demonstrates on what sort of journey the 'righteous side of life' can take us. Real people often bear a similarity to characters in fairy tales. With age, they can become noble and knowledgeable and it is this aspect that is hilarious in this fairy tale : Out in the country, a farmhouse could be seen which had a thatched roof on which moss and herbs were flourishing, a stork's nest sitting on the roof ridge (with the stork in it!), uneven house walls and low windows hiding behind an overhanging roof area (the overwhelming majority of these windows either had never been opened or could not be opened any more). A baker's oven leaps forward like a small, round belly and an elderberry bush leans over the fence to shield a puddle of water in which a duck and its ducklings paddle peacefully. The chained guard dog makes its presence felt too by barking at everybody. Such was the farmhouse in which a farmer lived with his wife and a number of other inhabitants.

This farmer and his wife were, on the one hand, poor. However, they didn't hesitate to bargain the little they had for something else. No matter what the farmer bartered, whether it seemed good or not, his wife always stuck by his decision, reassuring him, "Husband, you know best; I put all my trust in you." One day the farmer trotted to town on horseback after a hearty farewell and blessing from his wife. On his way, the farmer soon came across a cow which he regarded as charming and which gave him the idea of a wonderful source of milk.

The farmer talked the owner of the cow into a trade by explaining that a horse is worth more than a cow. This convinced the cow owner to agree.

Further along the road into town, a man with a well-fed, woolly sheep attracted the farmer's attention. "The green grass in the ditch on the side of the house path will do as food for the sheep and during winter we could keep it with us in the house as a pet," thought the farmer. Thus, he traded the cow for the sheep. Not long after on an intersection with another road, a heavy goose in the arms of its struggling owner caught the farmer's renewed attention. Quickly he made up his mind about the useful feathers and the tasty goose fat and so he bartered the sheep for the goose.

With every barter he made, the farmer knew that he had his wife's blessing and therefore enjoyed swapping ideas in his mind. They were on the whole mostly useful even if not entirely profitable. The closer the farmer came to town, the more people appeared on the road. The looks of the others made the farmer believe in his own importance so that he didn't stop looking around out of curiosity. This time, a funny looking hen on a lead in a potato field twinkled strikingly at him with one eye. It obviously wanted to be judged for its beauty and was looking for somebody to free it from its lead. At least in the eyes of the farmer, this chook was more beautiful than the one of the pastor. This helped him to make his decision quickly to swap the goose for the chook.

After most of the morning spent on foot, the farmer finally arrived at the outskirts of the town, where a pub on the roadside lured him in for a schnapps and bread. In the doorframe, an ostler with a sack over his shoulder blocked the entrance on his way out. Curiously, the farmer wanted to know what made the near bursting sack so heavy. "It's only rotten apples," the ostler replied. Memories from last year's poor apple crop on his own backyard trees made the farmer want these apples even though they were rotten.

The farmer's mother used to say, "No matter how little the crop, it's better kept than used up because ownership is a sign of wellbeing." The farmer thought about how his mum would have welcomed this lot of apples. This thought alone convinced the farmer to enter into the bargaining of the chook for the apples. Inside the pub, the bag of apples ended up leaning against the oven while the farmer joined the many guests at the tables. Not long after, a sizzling noise from the oven revealed that the apples in the bag had roasted from the oven's heat. "Your wife at home will teach you a lesson," the message came from the tables all around. The farmer responded, "My wife will only kiss me and never beat me because my mother has already said that whatever the father does is always right." One drinker responded,

"You can bet tonnes of gold coins that your wife is going to thrash you on delivery of these apples."

Another called out, "I'll bet you a bushel of gold!"

That being said, everybody agreed on it. Even the innkeeper made his car available so that the handful of people could go with the bag of rotten, sizzled apples to the farmer's house and see for themselves how the farmer would be welcomed. The farmer's wife had only praise for the husband when he told her about his dealings, "The horse for the cow would put cow's milk, butter and cheese on the table; the cow for the sheep needs less area to graze and would deliver the tasty sheep's milk and cheese plus woollen socks on top of it. "What about the change of the sheep for the goose?" asked the surrounding party. "We could fatten it up and have this year a Martin Goose. You are really good to me to think that far ahead," responded the farmer's wife.

But then the farmer said, "I couldn't stop bartering the goose for a chook." His wife laughed, "This is a great bargain. The chook would lay eggs and enrich us with a chook yard. This has always been one of my innermost wishes." The farmer finally finished with, "At the end however, I bartered the chook for a bag of rotten apples." The wife's response was quick, "Now I must kiss you and let you know that just when you went away, I wanted to get started on a really good meal of an omelette with chives except I had no chives. The neighbour was not prepared to help, instead arguing that not even one rotten apple worthy of swapping would grow in our garden. Now with that lot of apples I can give her more than she could have ever thought of. I know my husband is the best and here is a special kiss for you."

All this took place in the presence of the visitors from the pub who had come to witness this incredible course of events. One of the wealthy Englishmen had this to say, "I like that, going downhill and still maintaining steadfast cheerfulness. You have earned your bushel of gold for receiving kisses instead of a thrashing."

The moral of the story is that maintaining the 'righteous side of life' can, even under unpredictable conditions, lead to a predictably happy outcome. It was not only the Danish Christian Andersen who brought across practical life messages in his fairytales to his contemporaries in the 19th century. There was also Wilhelm Grimm, his German counterpart, who wrote "Hans in luck," a very similar fairytale about the righteous side of life succeeding in the end.

During the 19th century, people used to barter goods, especially those who had little or no money. What was then a barter of a cow for a sheep today involves something else for sure in industrialised countries. It is mainly that money has entered today's bargaining. However, it still delivers one and the same message: money can show only one side of life but there is much more waiting to be revealed which goes beyond the realm of money. Only maintenance of the 'righteous side of life' will prevail and carry us closer to contentment.

A more modern example shows how bartering today can lead to contentment. Swapping a used car with another one still leaves open the problematic side of paying the balance of the swap in money if the cars are of different value. We can never win; the problems always seem to involve a stiff-necked partner. However, if the 'righteous side of life' enables us to overcome the controversy of winning and losing through a more perceptive insight, then it is obviously more than just lucky or unlucky moments. We focus on something else rather than that which drives us up and down the speed bumps of life. Then we've reached that ground which can keep us on a relatively less controversial but definitely more contented side of life.

Having said this, we still have to make every effort to attain our goals and not just sit back and wait for it to happen. It is true that nothing has ever come from nothing and efforts towards a more personal freedom need to be ongoing. Why would this be worth striving for? Everything has its price both in wanted and unwanted forms. The one who gains a lot also carries burdens, which stress his vigilance away from just his few individual concerns. Confusion can then set in, opening the door to unforeseeable 'games' of control.

We all no doubt see such circumstances as uncertainty, worry, anxiety, aggression, sickness, incapacity, sick social behaviour and much more. These can slowly work their way into daily lives, sidetracking the individual as well as society as a group. The more we strive for, the more attention must be paid to staying on the main road, with all side roads feeding 'traffic' into it. A road seems an apt analogy for life's passage, creating a very realistic environment in which today's 'traffic' moves quickly, mainly to gain distance while many aim to overtake others. The less distance covered on such a 'road' the less likely one is to meet junctions and consequently can better defend a 'righteous road'. This is because there is less 'traffic interference' from upcoming junctions.

By travelling far on life's road, there are more people with whom whose motives one has to compete. However, going a short distance brings less competition, enabling the individual to stay less compromised. Collective and individual 'wants' as well as 'needs' lead to the question of adaptation and, most of all, how long can this be upheld without side effects emerging which lead to a negative outcome.

While the symbolic 'road' on which we travel indicates our responsibility for, and interaction with, the traffic, there is also the analogy of a 'river' that carries us all along. On reflection, a river determines the course of travel and we have to be vigilant to avoid being stranded on its banks, cut off from the main stream. Does the 'mainstream' have the answers to how the 'righteous side of life' enhances a 'simple life'? Probably not, because in the mainstream our contacts are close enough to unleash the inevitable fights for a better survival. Whereas outside the mainstream, in tranquil waters closer to the riverbanks, the river's waters allow anchorage time, time to catch up with ourselves and the environment we are living in.

The rushing forces of the mainstream carry everything quickly down its course. Everything is bound to follow this course, leaving very little else for the individual 'boat' to consider. It's simply a life in the fast lane where speed frenzy, addiction to change and challenges of obstacles all beg attention, diverting us from the real life issues. These issues are important and allow us to identify ourselves as individuals in actions and creativity. One can also comprehend better and largely take control for oneself. Only from there can we start focussing effectively on the people surrounding us. This might involve helping, socialising or even distancing ourselves in time in order to protect our identity, but it definitely should not be by means of warfare.

It is important to get one's own house in order before we reveal ourselves to the rest of the world. Then exchanges can begin, of which an individual learns more from others how to gain his/her own 'righteous side of life'. It is only in the contest with challenges that we gain strength in our own conviction. Alternately, we can lose confidence in ourselves, which should be regarded as a call to go back to the 'drawing board' and adjust to emerging changes.

It is mainly in this field of exchanges that the 'righteous side of life' can be found. Sometimes it's because of raging individual battles for personal freedom and not just existing in isolation. It is not without reason that it is said that life can be a battle. However, it is in the battle itself that it is crucial how we fight. With aggression, we almost certainly call up counter-aggression, which can lead to the ominous consequences of fights and war. The 'righteous side of life' constantly sought in conflicting situations is an important road sign towards a 'simple life'. This cannot happen by sitting back and doing nothing.

CHAPTER 13

Taking Advantage of Evil Practices

As we all know, the world doesn't run in a single 'lane'. Rather, there are many more 'lanes' which carry our 'traffic' to different destinations, including to those we are not necessarily actively pursuing. One such 'lane' might carry the name, right of advantage, which could lead to 'evil practices'. Fast traffic in the 'overtaking lane' will certainly lend the right to the lucky few to use conditions to their advantage, reaching a destination earlier than the mainstream, if everything goes to plan. The emphasis is on 'if' and herein starts the point of discussion.

Consider this more or less daily occurrence: our modern life is based on advantage taking, ahead of other people, to the extent that in our drive for bigger and better, our attention becomes distracted away from life-facts. Who would argue about somebody investing his or her savings from hard-earned money in an institution, which promises the advantage of increasing the amount paid in? All you have to do is watch and wait as your 'fortune' grows. Which avenues such an investment can take can vary enormously. The current financial market has demonstrated more than once that investment remains an open game. Much is usually said, but much more *happens,* and it is only much later that a business is verified as either righteous or evil.

Only recently in 2008/2009, the world experienced a wake-up call on an unprecedented scale. The value of money has gone downhill worldwide partly due to 'evil practices'. To date, there is still nobody who wants to, or even can, call the shots about what really went wrong. What caused the whole world to go bankrupt all of a sudden, taking individuals down that extremely rough road with their savings? One fact cannot be denied. For too long, 'evil practices' have taken advantage through undercover operations on the money market but not on the labour market. As a consequence, the labour market received its 'bashing' too.

All the commonplace aspects of life such as trust, reliability, promises, belief, can be hijacked into the territory of evil practices. This is especially so if control mechanisms are less effective than in the past. Here is the crucial point of control being overcome by profit seeking - the world has declared profit to be its 'sacred cow' and everything is subjugated to this demand. In this world, 'liberalism' and 'control' have become antagonists which belong to one 'family', unleashing typical family disputes all in the name of profit seeking. More liberalism can create more profit advises the 'smart' economy adviser. However, this will only happen at the expense of the wider public, which is told that when liberalism flourishes, everybody will get his or her share of profit. Such one-sided, advantage taking has been evident in the presence of 'evil practices' which have been allowed to establish themselves with priority given to profit making.

A call for better control comes only *after* the 'economy-child' has already fallen into the 'well' again at the expense of the wider public. Control measures will then contribute to the account of a reduced profit which liberalism then tries to rebuild to its advantage. Such have been and still are the economical cycles. What goes up has also to come down again. If human greed however, would agree to live on smaller profits, the antagonists of liberalism and control would lose the sting of a downturn in the economy and establish instead a benefit of more stability.

One essential core-problem is to be found in the segregation of economic activities from real, productive activities and the accompanying services. Currently, these play a disproportionate role within societies. It is mainly these accompanying services that are responsible for hijacking others' efforts by turning the profit 'screw' to see what it can endure. This kind of evil, reckless behaviour has been around forever and it is doubtful whether human greed will want to, or even actually can, foster the necessary changes towards more stable conditions in a hurry. It seems that there is no choice other than to live with the 'ups' and 'downs' while having reached one of these positions. It can only teach us repeated lessons of how to rediscover the opposite effect.

These are some of the advantages of evil practices. They can flourish only until wake-up calls remind us once more of the better road to travel. This road leads closer to our 'Simple Life' by saving us the excesses of the 'ups' and 'downs' in life. Belonging to something, hanging on to it, can give us a sense of belonging. However, this membership might also lead to being caught up in the daily battle. Here, the more advantage-seeking that takes place under the umbrella of an organisation, the closer the risk is.

But just what would make a practice 'evil' in financial terms? Generally speaking, the so-called financial avenues of investments are usually explicable as long as they do not diversify into financial 'sidetracks', where direct accountability is hampered if not completely obscured. Then, a direct link with the original capital input becomes more difficult to control, thereby opening the floodgates to 'evil practices'. The financial crisis in 2008/2009 demonstrated this, suddenly throwing the entire world into economic chaos. The more cautious investors did not follow blindly or naively into advantageous propositions. Consequently, they were more likely not to have burnt their fingers. Ultimately, we are paying in life for something we cannot really comprehend sufficiently.

To build on one's own efforts is the longer but more secure road to success. There is no real shortcut to vague trends, often via scams, in economic activities. Relying on other economic activities on the other hand, looks a bit like a gambling game in which we can be condemned to play a preset role. However, there is always the other side: that of personal freedom, which allows us to make individual decisions. Working on this individual side of the equation is a certain pointer towards a 'Simple Life'. Certainly, the downsides of life cannot be completely avoided but we can learn our lessons and not necessarily continue along the gambling route.

Recently, there was reported on the news an incident in which two University students had successfully utilised an 'evil practice' for gain. However, as the outcome demonstrated it was not for long. Here too the adage proved to be right: a jug falls into the well only until it breaks. The two students thought they had found the easy answer to their money needs. A copy of the key to the parking meters in and around the city centre somehow found its way into their possession so they could take advantage of an 'evil practice'. Daily, before the official money collection from the meters took place, one of the two students would collect the money, which, even over a short time, amounted to a considerable sum. In the end, it wasn't the parking meters, which brought the venture down but something else further down the line.

In the past, a local bank had regularly received the fairly large number of coins from the meters. The two students considered it less conspicuous to use the unattended automatic coin-counting machine inside the bank. This kind of daily visit, around the same time each day, did not go unnoticed. Eventually, somebody in the bank was alerted and began to look a bit closer at what was going on. The account where the money was deposited showed a respectable fortune being amassed, already surpassing one million dollars. For a student account, it certainly wasn't the norm. As well as this, the low revenues from the official meter collection simultaneously sparked suspicion, despite there being no visible break-in marks on the parking meters. Both the bank and the officially appointed meter collector advised the police of the suspicious circumstances. This led to an investigation by the police and the perpetrators were quickly apprehended *in flagrante*. The dream of a luxurious life had come to an end.

Anybody with common sense would have thought that the legal arm would impose appropriate sentences upon such an evil practice. However, we are living in a different world today. The two perpetrators argued that there were extenuating circumstances and pleaded for community service rather than jail time and this was the verdict handed down. To some extent, such a verdict could be understood, but the students were in fact 'legal science' students and obviously played the system.

What hope is there for the legal profession in the future, if the legal ranks are going to consist of delinquents who offended in their early lives? Would the rules apply here too: 'a crow doesn't peck out the eye of another one' and 'birds of a feather flock together'? The future of course will tell whether the outcome proves to be for the better or the worse! The advantage that came of this 'evil practice' was, in any case, short-lived, robbing the student adventurers of a future based on a 'Simple Life'. Whether they re-offended or not, the point is that not only *old* habits, but also *early* habits, will die hard.

We have almost become blasé about an environment congested with advertising logos and images. These advertisements all promise something, the core of which is discovered only later on. In times of fast changes, lasting qualities can lose their originality by becoming subordinated to these ever present changes. These changes are, in a sense, in opposition to tradition, the patron of long lasting quality. In such a context, the more trustworthy an advantage seems to the consumer, the more the consumer is hooked on it. Relatively short warranty concessions aim to give consumers an additional advantage, just in case it should be needed. Competition for instance, in the car industry has gradually extended warranty concessions but not without binding consumers to tighter conditions. Regular services within warranty periods are subject to these conditions. The lasting message is, "The money we don't get upfront, we will get off you later in a number of small instalments."

All kinds of money loans for all sorts of consumer products belong to the same family of enticing advantages. Many people are lured into buying a car, a house or a smaller item where one's own money is not a real issue any more. Companies put an extended time for payment and the customer gets that sense of ownership without having paid out one cent. In return, the client has only to adhere to the company's rules and keep on paying. Evil practices are conveniently kept well hidden: not evident at first glance but often there in fine print on the back of a contract requiring expert interpretation. Later, when these obligations are discovered by a less than satisfied customer, a wake-up call will tell them that it is always the customer who is left 'holding the baby'. The company on the other hand is in 'clover', rarely if ever missing out on its profit. Here, practices leading to one side have to deal with 'baby nappies' while the other side reaps the benefits. They are the ones that stand for 'evil'.

Curiously, there is not much evident difference between the appearances of an 'evil practice' and that of an honest one. The cosmetic camouflage of words can cover pretty much the same ground. A quotation of Goethe, the German Shakespeare, demonstrates this: "Words battle with superiority." The smarter one better understands that it is important to hide his weaker arguments, leaving others vulnerable to undercover 'evil practices'. This is the outcome when the less aware participant cannot at first glance recognise the hidden arguments. A good touchstone for those wanting to avoid becoming the victim of 'evil practices' has always been, take your time; don't rush; look at something from more than one side. Evil practices have no reward; only the good ones do.

Again, my own version of a Finnish fairytale ably demonstrates this and is a good teacher of life's lessons. Two brothers went out into the world to seek their fortune. The elder brother went first in a cart pulled by a horse. Soon after leaving home, on the stony road, desperate ants signalled to the rushing horse and cart to stop until the ant family could pass across the road safely. The brother's response was, "I've no time; why should I waste my precious time with such little, insignificant creatures? I am in a hurry for something much more important, seeking my fortune. Get out of my way or I'll crush all of you under my cart wheels," and the older brother did so in his great rush.

Further on, green patchy grass covered the road because of the little traffic that moved there. For that reason, a duck had built its nest in the middle of the road, fostering a most promising clutch of eggs. On arrival of the cart, the duck in a jolt of dismay urged the older brother to stop and allow the duck to move the eggs out of the way. "No duck will stop me from reaching my goal. First come, first served, is the rule and this is what you deserve." The eggs too were crushed under the rushing wheels of the cart.

Continuing on, dense grassland overgrew the road. Here a great titmouse flew near the brother's ear, begging a lift because its wings were not strong any more. "You stay where you are. Get off; I've no time to listen to bird tattle; I'm pursuing my fortune." The great titmouse retreated to the bush to sing a sorry song.

Journeying on, the older brother arrived in the King's city, wasting no time and going straight to the Court in the hope of gaining good fortune by marrying the King's daughter. The King welcomed the new suitor immediately leading him right into the courtyard in front of a big heap of mixed rye and wheat. "If you separate the rye from the wheat in the coming night, you will have fulfilled the first task on the way to becoming my son-in-law. However, if you do not succeed, my executioner will wait for you." The boy took on the task, realising early enough that the task was beyond his calibre. The older brother's mind turned to how useful the ants in their great numbers would have been now. He rued crushing the ant family. The older brother could not of course fulfil the task unaided and the executioner's axe became his fate.

One year later, the younger brother went out to seek his fortune. When he arrived with his cart and horse at the spot on the road with the ants, he calmly answered the ants' call to wait with the horse and cart until the entire ant family had crossed the road. The duck too, he allowed to nurse the eggs until they hatched. Finally, he invited the titmouse, "Come with me. Let's travel together. It's much nicer to have somebody to talk to."

In the company of the titmouse, the younger brother arrived at the King's city in order to ask for his daughter's hand in marriage. Faced with the same task of separating the rye from the wheat, he was spared the fate of his older brother because the entire ant family came to help him with the task. The King could not believe his eyes when he saw the rye and wheat carefully separated into two piles.

"You've to prove yourself to me again. Another task is waiting for you, the second of three. The key of my treasury has fallen to the bottom of the sea. Dive down and bring it back and I will consider your request for my daughter's hand more favourably." The duck came to the rescue of the younger brother and delivered the key from the bottom of the sea.

"When you can fulfil the third and last task, the reward will be yours. You must pick out my daughter and then she is yours." All the pretty young girls of the King's city lined up in one row in the courtyard, waiting and laughing and all dressed the same. The titmouse flew to the younger brother's ear whispering, "I will fly to the shoulder of the King's daughter so that you know which one she is." The happy couple lived contentedly together for many years, evidence of the moral of this fairytale, 'Taking advantage of evil practices does not lead to good luck, a good life or a simple life.'

The fairytale's origin is Finland, a country that has a rich heritage of such 'wisdoms'. Despite the fact that fairytales look back in time, their wisdom does not change with time, continuing to evoke invariable life rules that also lead to a 'Simple Life'. Humankind has always longed for simplicity in life with varying degrees of success. This is because that as we err in our actions, we also defeat our innermost longings.

Taking advantage of evil practices is another human error, which takes us along the road of a difficult life. It is difficult because the key for simplicity has been lost. By not taking a step back from the pursuit of greedy, self-centred lives aren't we 'playing' a superior role above all the other living forms? Don't we do this at a collective level as well as at an individual level? A more humble assessment of ourselves will not tarnish our glory. All will have a modest end anyway, so why not seek out the password for a 'Simple Life'. Hopefully, by studying the diversity of ways to seek the 'Simple Life', each participant in 'life's journey' will find a way that suits them.

CHAPTER 14

Being Endowed with Talents and Intellect

Humans, just like all other living forms - plants or animals - all respond differently to the same conditions and treatment. What holds the clue to such a basic fact? Is it talent: that natural affinity some humans demonstrate when meeting things like music, art, science etc in everyday life? Or is it intellect: that intelligence and brain power endowed to us by our genetic background? What is more likely is that we advance both individually and collectively out of unilateral mediocrity and into advancement through a combination of both. Personally, envisaged goals are usually only met by drawing on both talent and intellect.

Similarly, there is not much argument against life experience being our best teacher, as only real life situations will make or break individual talent and intellect. Without the endurance test of life, nothing we do can claim any real value. A challenge only makes the end results, the outcome, more fulfilling. Achieving for the sake of achieving in itself would be fruitless if not put to the test of life's anvil or life's grinding stone.

Back in Greek history, *"talanton,"* and in Latin *"talantus,"* stood for personal values representing initially a 'sum of money' whereas intellect comes from the Latin '*intellectus*' meaning understanding. Even in today's world, talent and intellect depend on each other in order to make the individual prosper in life in a well-balanced manner. In isolation, neither talent nor intellect can rise above mediocrity. Only when talent feeds on intellect can they emerge together in a strong bond.

Let us look at talent and intellect separately in order to understand what the origin of each is. Talent is said to represent values of inherited ability as well as developed nature, from which an individual can draw a strong bargaining position with other people on condition that the talent has been recognised. If talent is fostered and encouraged by others there is a much greater chance of success than if the individual has been left on his/her own.

What is talent as it is recognised by individuals? One way of looking at it is as the ability to learn better and more efficiently. This can be in any field: music, languages, practical skills, theoretical skills, fantasy, coordinated body movement for ball games, swimming, maths, endurance, quick crisis reaction, modest exercising, social skills such as gentle, smart behaviour, even the stricture of good manners, persuasive and constructive support of others. However, there are also 'negative' talents, which also thrive in nature's realm: cunning, deliberate cheating, misleading, showing off and much more.

Keeping talent hidden like a 'personal jewel' does no good to anybody, including the individual. A talent has to come out into the testing field of real life with other talents in order to become recognised as such. Here inevitably, rules do apply where people meet, regardless of the purpose. One important rule has remained into modern times despite continuously being questioned - discipline. Without appropriate discipline, talent cannot fully prosper. Discipline is a majority agreement among people, which is necessary for individuals to coexist peacefully.

Apart from a simple definition of discipline, it is itself better understood outside in the practical world where it reflects upon daily activities. Good discipline leads to winning at rugby, soccer, tennis, any game in fact. It shows in the attaining of good school marks, persevering with sport to master challenges in which winning not necessarily becomes the exclusive goal, climbing a mountain, setting goals and meeting targets, recovering from ill health, getting along well with others. Plainly, survival is reliant to a certain extent on discipline. Poor discipline eventually results in not reaching targets and as a consequence failure to win a majority endorsement. It is also well known and accepted that a favourite sports person or celebrity who dares to disappoint will face people's disapproval. Others' expectations basically can't be met without the celebrity's understanding of disciplinary measures and the part it plays in their success.

Where does discipline start? From early on in life, it is passed on, hopefully, from parent to child, from mentor to mentee in order to learn how to use it successfully. Lack of discipline has long-term effects on the natural talent source. A degree of adopted discipline, when trying to develop natural talent, determines the developmental capacity of a talent. Discipline, responding to and applied to a talent at a high level, is an essential prerequisite for experiencing real progress. Music is a good example of discipline versus talent. A symphony orchestra is probably the most outstanding disciplinary interaction of all expressions of musical talent. It is equally important however in any sport or in written and verbal expressions addressing other people in which discipline is the entire 'leitmotiv'.

Little or no discipline ensures that any expression of talent will fail, creating room then for the ones who have the passion and discipline to succeed despite some talent shortcomings. This then is a case of wasted talent. Action in life remains, in any case, imperative, whether with or without natural talent. These proverbs paint a supportive picture: 'no one is born a master' and 'no pain, no gain'.

Talent can give the individual advantages over someone with little talent. Certainly, everybody has some degree of talent but it is only if the entrusted talent is nurtured from the cradle, recognised and developed, that it can grow to be a formidable success. Gifted talent has the upper hand over many competitors by making it possible to reach recognisable performances in a shorter time. Talented lazybones however, do not succeed in the long run if they are competing with those of little natural talent but with voracious discipline. Consistent effort with a capacity to listen also to nature's voice will demonstrate the importance of talent and discipline.

Nature does compensate humans in many ways for what we consider our shortcomings. This rarely happens on its own, as nature wants us to lend a helping hand in the 'compensation case'. Obvious examples are for instance when deafness is compensated for by improved visual sensation or, blindness by better hearing. Moreover, a missing body limb can empower a person to compensate so that a foot takes over what missing hands cannot perform any more. We have all heard of people writing and even painting with a foot or a mouth.

Much in nature is actually based on compensation, a call for us to recognise and give nature this helping hand rather than taking shortcuts such as those provided by some drugs, for instance. Here, the use of intellect is important. The reason is that, with the approval and disapproval of measures concerning people, one has to be able to produce an understanding, which again largely depends on a performance arising from talent and not from talent-enhancing drugs.

Having looked at the impact of talent, what then is intellect and how does it affect the road to the 'Simple Life'? Like talent, intellect is evident early, from the cradle even. Education from outside the individual impacts on the natural intellect evident from birth. It is a common proposition that the underlying basis of intellect is invested in us even before birth. No question remains however about the fact that intellect is formed and developed over an entire lifespan. It starts with an early dependency on the family to kick start the process which, during life, teaches us to stand up to challenges from outside sources. Under such a course of events, intellect should indicate a balance between nature and nurture – yes, we are born with a degree of intellect but it can also develop further from interaction with the world around us.

Failure to address even minute disciplinary issues during early childhood can have far-reaching effects on the future course of the individual. In other words, what starts off small – whether it is a course of action that is right, wrong or in the grey area in between - will develop into something correspondingly bigger over time. Such is the nature of intellect though; it is mostly the individual's desire to prevent a collision course with the majority of other people.

In their search for intellectual maturity young people are, by nature, impatient. They are constantly testing the bounds of acceptance into the adult world. Derailment is always a strong possibility and many reach the point of no return in their pursuit of the adults' world of mainstream conventions. However, as long as that point is not crossed, intellect can benefit from such testing experiences, which is often the case with bright children. Unfortunately, with many adolescents these intellectual forays into the adult world often turn out to be misguided attempts. How many times do parents throw up their hands, exclaiming in amazement, "Why do our children give us so many headaches?" This is a common occurrence on the road to a 'Simple Life' and it is important not to abandon such a pilgrimage. However, hope for a return to normality should be given priority over the abandonment of such efforts, because the consequent losses in human relations weigh heavier than purely materialistic ones. Life's journey, and not a quick coffee table chat in comfort, is the only way to establish this imperative truth.

Intellect, what is it good for? Although it is often referred to as a commonplace thing in daily conversations, it is doubtful whether many have a near enough picture of what intellect really is. Intellect has gone through changes in history, just as societies have done, by lifting the veil of ignorance about new territories from time to time. What originally constituted a move away from a declared convention only became re-established in a new 'gown' afterwards so that its intellectual owners could still approach the ladder of success.

Such established intellect however is in stark contrast to real intellect in which nature demands survival in competitions. A light at the end of the intellect tunnel is also a guide to a 'Simple Life' if the tunnel passage is manageable. This means that somewhere along the line the 'wheat' has been separated from the 'chaff' with regard to intellect right through to individual ranks.

Firstly, in our 'life-boat', we tend to take on board many impediments to intellect until life's voyage teaches us the essentials by testing us with 'raging waters'. The less ballast we carry, the more we will be able to reap the benefit of fewer intellectual essentials. No obliging measure of intellect can link individuals; rather it creates a distance between them. If we are truly honest in our observations, there are as many intellect levels as there are individuals. That which is great for one individual can be much less so for another one. Here again is a pointer between essential and non-essential issues for the individual on the road to a 'Simple Life'.

Intellect should likewise never hurt our well-being; otherwise, it couldn't endure the scrutiny of its true goal in life i.e. being further enhanced by talent. In order to get onto the road to the 'Simple Life', both talent and intellect have to be addressed simultaneously. A measure of inherited or developed talent is in direct relation to intellect capacity. Intellect is essentially 'good', while still requiring ultimately the sanctioning of others. In isolation, this 'good ship' is doomed to 'go down' with all hands.

How is intellect recognisable, individually and/or collectively? In order to answer this question it is helpful also to establish the kind of intellect that exists. The first of these is 'established' intellect, the second is 'false' intellect and finally there is 'purpose' intellect.

Natural intellect draws directly from individual talent and is a direct student-teaching outcome, which is passed on, certified and ready to be tested in the world of real action. It is drawn not only from lessons taught but also from the ability to make decisions that prove to be the better ones in a variety of situations. Often it is recognisable in an additional student-learning process on the job.

False intellect can be related to a display, for instance, in which the focus is mainly on visual presentation. It is probably less challenging mentally. In another example, someone's proud boasting can often be of a superficial nature, lacking any great degree of intellect. Moreover, it can stand to reason that a lie can also shift intellect into false territory. In a sense, every intellectual expression that hasn't received enough foundation work, will find itself in limbo sooner rather than later. Ultimately, on whatever performance-level, our peers will judge this type of intellect on its merit.

Purpose intellect is a 'fabrication' of facts as found in advertisements, propaganda and with the people handling it. Accuracy is not a prominent marker of purpose intellect either. Rather, in order to catch people's attention, it does cut short extended, more thorough fact-findings, which could spark unwanted or difficult questions. The emphasis is on speed and emotional impact to win over people so that they become more easily satisfied and do not have to rack their own brains. Under the cover of 'facilitation' in inter-human relations, many people get hooked on to false purpose intellect results. This is not a passport to a 'Simple Life' as the principles of simplicity have been neglected. There is no honesty, openness, circumspection, moderation, positive acting and thinking.

Talent and intellect almost certainly will interact in today's world. Very few things in this world are wrought by intellect alone; they too work in accordance with talent, luck, timing and chance. There are many examples in modern times of just how the two might interact in our lives.

For instance, current Formula 1 racing driver Sebastian Vettel, only 22 years old, constantly challenges the experts in the motor racing world. Talent and self-driven determination have enabled him to cut short the usual learning process and period gaining experience, which such extreme challenges demand in Formula 1 racing. Somewhere along the line, somebody must have made the 'right' decision to introduce this 'young blood' into the ranks of the previously successful racing teams, setting new standards in the world of achievements. It does however, appear to take some time before such methods push progress further. Usually it is the well-known and experienced sportsman rather than the new star arriving 'out of the blue', who will win the accolades. This doesn't happen only in motorcar racing.

The tennis world recently experienced a surprise when a largely unknown Argentinean pushed both crowned champions, Federer and Nadal, out of the first ranks in the 2009 US Open. Motor racing and tennis are just two of a vast number of publicly popular events in which this anomaly exists. What these surprise performers all have in common is that only few show the long-term effort and experience usually required to be a winner. The vast majority can sit back in relative comfort trying to catch up with an excitement, which these few others produce.

'Surprise performers' especially, are by nature endowed with a degree of aggression in their behaviour which is reflected in strong self-confidence, enabling them to dominate others in survival situations. Aggression, as part of a talent search, can dominate intellect. It is only when individual experiences are balanced against this drive for superiority that greatness can occur. Experience is part of a learning process in weighing up risk-taking against caution. Sooner or later, most of us settle down in life with less risk taking as our experience grows. It is, and always has been, mainly the privilege of the young in taking risks to find out how far natural talent can carry them.

In the vernacular, people commonly state, "You can't teach talent," adding however that this is where effective learning starts. In addition, becoming the 'extraordinary' player can never be achieved by the majority of people except in their dreams or as spectators. Much of it awakens exemplars out of which another 'surprise performer' can be born. But more often than not, a failure to reach this extraordinary level of talent is the norm.

Those who aim high should not forget that we all have to come down again to a level of sustainability, different for, but inherent to, each individual. A simple example is the climbing of a mountain which in hindsight shows that the descent is always more difficult. Good preparation has never been quick, except maybe for that 'surprise' performer. However, not allowing for that 'descent' makes the path towards a 'Simple Life' much more difficult. A fool is recognised by flying to a height from which the descent is either impossible or extremely dangerous. The 'surprise' performer is like a lonely star high above everybody else, a situation very different from that of the mainstream. Much more than what the public is aware of still happens in everybody's daily lives and yet it has still turned more or less into a race of 'super' performers.

In families, it is readily acknowledged that children can be endowed with either talent, intellect or both to very different degrees. It is here where early practices for future careers are set. After-school schedules need parental guidance to assist in varied tasks including school homework. Children, of course, would love to put off homework to pursue other interests even for a short time. However, this time easily becomes extended so that time for homework has shrunk considerably.

Paul, Peter and Gloria are the children of a teacher. As usual, the parents want to see their offspring advance in life, often further than they themselves have achieved. Paul does his homework usually late at night with seemingly little effort and always brings home excellent school marks. It is easy to think that he must be the talent in the family, obviously not easily accepted by his brother and sister. They, on the other hand, have to spend quite a bit more time not only on their school homework but also in catching up on other school subjects - Peter with foreign languages and Gloria with science.

All three children pass through school with varying degrees of success and at different times. Paul is admitted straight to University, whereas Peter and Gloria choose the more practical, hands-on professions. Only in the years to come does a clearer picture emerge of how differently talent and intellect can work in life. Paul, the declared 'talent', achieved his formal qualifications and had a career promising a good future and secure employment opportunities. On the other hand, at first glance Peter and Gloria seemed to be not quite as successful. However, both reached stability in their lives through long-term employment. Such an outcome could be regarded favourable despite its inherent differences.

A very different picture can develop when talent and intellect go astray in environs other than the accustomed ones. Simply being in the wrong place at the wrong time can determine a course of events and ensure the individual ends up on the wrong track. Look at an accident for instance. What would we see this as - talent or intellect failure? In addition, what about the teenager or aspirant who suddenly turns away from parental and educational guidance to get hooked on that downhill path to crime and addiction. This life might lead to alcohol abuse, drug abuse, 'alternative lifestyles', disobedience to any form of discipline, resorting to crime, to following adverse or perverse models which deviate from the majority convention. Who is then to blame for this individual's failure to meet the expectations of others? Where has talent and intellect been left in any of these cases?

Can we afford to remain silent and let events conveniently take their course until they turn into something in stark opposition to talent and intellect? Somehow, we are all linked together in our destinies, even in the rejection of society's 'failures'. We are never set free from mutual responsibilities to our fellow human creatures. Talent and intellect should connect or associate us whereas, in isolation, they disassociate us from each other. Questions of isolation in said matters never arise from just one person's opinion but rather between opposing parties. As a matter of course, individual and collective opposition can have a long history, starting off usually in familiar territory. Finally, the opposition is recognised in unfamiliar territory, where the transition into broader intellectual issues has not been given enough attention.

It has also to be said that everybody has some natural talent, which has to be recognised by others only in order to advance towards intellect. Failure to recognise talent on any societal level is not only the main source of opposition but it is also a direction away from a 'Simple Life'. Reconciliation with conflict in life has then missed reaching individuals and consequently the communities in which they are living. It is so simple to grant recognition to others if only we are prepared to step back a little from our self-declared intellect in order to allow others to join in a talent search.

To conclude this, look at intellect and talent, an own fable by the author about a fox and a raven ably demonstrates the premises discussed : On a cold winter's day, a raven intercepted a fox in a white snow-covered, open field, a fair distance away from the protection of the forest.

"Hello Mister Fox, where has Talent left you today?" came from the black raven just before he found a resting place on top of a lonely, wooden post.

"Times are tough lately. How does Intellect get you through this winter and into next summer?" Mister Fox questioned Mr Raven.

"I'm not worried like you on the ground because from the air I can see more and further than you can."

"This is what your Intellect tells you but you come down to the ground and you'll see where you are left with your fantastic vision. You won't have much of a chance down here with me."

"I could say the same thing. You try your luck in the air just once," said the raven.

"Ah, this is not right. I don't like your objection. Let's put your Intellect to the test against my Talent and see which of us catches a feed first," responded the fox.

"No problem; I'm already off for my next tasty feed," and the raven gently lifted off the wooden post with a calm wing stroke.

However, the deep, fresh snow from last night considerably slowed down Mr Fox on the ground. "Why should I wreck myself in the snow for a lousy raven? I'd rather hide and wait for my nose to tell me of the scent of a poor, lost hare. I'm not running after small mice like that raven does."

As time went on, Mr Fox thought that, as Mr Raven hasn't turned up yet with his catch, there was no point in rushing. Hunger however registered increasingly in the fox's stomach, which he ignored to the best of his ability. "That black-winged rival can't pull my leg in the air," the lonely fox convinced himself. Just a moment later, in the air above, flapping wings diverted Mr Fox's attention.

"Look what I've got for dinner. What have you managed so far?" crowed Mr Raven from above the fox.

Mr Fox didn't want to see himself shamed. Neither did he want to let the raven see him defeated. "Ah, this bit of stuff you've caught is no good for me. I need a proper feed which demands time to be delivered."

"Anyway, I have my dinner for the day despite having to search near and far for it. Your Talent didn't bring you far in your search. I'm off to settle for the night in the forest trees. Good luck with your talented nose!"

"You black Devil! Don't you dare annoy me. I know what I'm doing; you better beware that I don't get you for dinner together with your little starter-meal," exclaimed Mr Fox.

"Go ahead and try your luck while I'm off into my territory. Good night, Mr Fox."

Beaten down by such humiliation, Mr Fox put his bushy tail between his legs and crept to his nearby burrow in the ground, trying to forget how he had ended up so hungry.

The message of the story is, 'No pain, no gain,' regardless of talent or intellect. 'One should rather keep the sparrow in the hand instead of trying to get hold of the pigeons on the roof'.

CHAPTER 15

Sharing Life with Less Gifted Individuals

The initial question, which arises about this issue is, why *should* life be shared with less gifted individuals? Certainly, the next question would then be, what purpose does it serve? If we are true to ourselves, this is the mirror to our way of thinking. Asking questions cannot be regarded as a necessarily bad thing. What is bad however is the little thought behind some opinions.

Let us focus on the 'why' first. Whom are the people asking such questions, be it openly or in private only to himself or herself? Is it everybody? And if not, who are these individuals? To be honest, we all more or less think first of covering our own interests before getting concerned too much about others. This is also considered 'smart' and who in today's world wouldn't want to be considered 'smart'? If everybody was 'smart', would it mean that there would be no lesser-gifted individuals around anymore? If everybody claimed to be 'smart', it simply would not compute because, by the very nature of the beast, 'smart' *needs* the other side for comparison – the less gifted individuals who have been 'outsmarted' have gone missing.

In other words, 'smart' people can only exist when on another side there are enough people to be 'outsmarted'.

What or who is commonly regarded as 'fair' or 'not fair'? Would they match the description of foot soldiers, luck pushers, glitterati or draught horses? 'Fair' is usually claimed by that side of society, which doesn't tire of laying claims to advantage taking within a hierarchy established for that individual purpose. Climbing that particular ladder of the establishment, one will find confirmation of what has eventually been left behind: the so-called 'crumbs'. Everybody else who claims something better than these 'crumbs' finds himself subjected to fighting outside the establishment guidelines.

For such reasons, people do fight during the course of their lives. Fighting has become one of the last 'instincts' with which nature has endowed us, making intellect the underdog. Fighting has never been an action of intellect, rather a sign of intellect gone missing. Intellect is the balancing power, which hopefully oversees life's controversies so that we do not run blindly in a single direction. Blind running in a single direction only leads to the dead end road out of which only renewed fighting can move us further.

Out in the 'real world', everybody is admittedly fighting for something. Does it mean the one who is fighting better is the one who is better off? Less fighting and more circumspection for people who can fight less effectively, is the intelligent life choice. It is only a matter of time before the plight of those less effective fighters catches up with the successful front-runners. Then, the gifted and the less gifted will find themselves trapped together, wittingly or unwittingly, trying to get off the dead end road, which unfortunately still involves fighting to this day.

This leads to the answer to the question of why we should share life with less gifted individuals. Sooner or later, in often unpredictable ways, somebody else's plight is going to involve the rest of us. This begs the question, 'Of what benefit is it to share life with less gifted individuals?' The freedom of others is in real terms also our freedom. **The less we care about others, no matter what their level of intellect might be, the more opposition there is to either group building a worthwhile life from which to enjoy personal freedoms.** Societies have, in the past, become reenergised from a broader, vital base of societal participants and never selectively. This has become known today as 'people power'.

It needs to be said also that no rule can last by ignoring this 'people power'. Such has been the dominance of 'people power' throughout history, that a mixture of individuals on varying levels, not exclusively gifted or less gifted, have come forward expressing common desires for action. A gifted individual should also be recognised by the less gifted ones unless it would seem that the gifted individual is guilty of self-praise. In return, a gifted individual finds an echo with the less gifted ones if dialogue has kept enough doors open. This is actually the recipe for success with people.

Another aspect should be addressed as well. There is a moral aspect in sharing life with less gifted individuals. The question of 'what is it good for?' might be raised here as well. A number of people will probably ask, what is a 'moral aspect'? A 'moral' is a broad consent regulating inter-human relations, which are understood by a majority of people and upheld accordingly. 'Moral' engages all human expressions and activities starting with very basic necessary conduct, such as dressing instead of being naked, keeping up personal cleanliness as well as more sophisticated understandings of mutual decency, politeness, help, respect and much more. Here, 'moral' relating to less gifted individuals finds its home base also in mutual responsibilities. It's not good enough to want to succeed by going it alone and leaving fellow creatures too far behind. Aspiring success is like climbing a mountain. With strength, a will and everything else that is needed to secure the difficult ascent, others have to be on the team as well.

An African proverb presents this reflection: "If you want to go fast, you have to go it alone: if you want to go far, you have to go it together." The lonely way is here the more difficult one as the challenger faces provocations unsupported. He who surmounts those provocations alone in life can claim the resultant benefits for himself. However, that position at the top can be very lonely.

On the other side, the risks can become an incessant burden all the way. Every individual is to a degree gifted, but not always easily recognised as such from an outside observation. Working together has the benefit of teamwork in which more than one level of gifted individual can come forward and assist to help ease a single burden. For such a reason, a team can go further than an individual can because they not only share the benefits but more importantly, they share the burden too. This eases that crucial load for everybody, allowing one to continue for longer.

Such attention, shared with varying levels of gifted individuals, is regarded as a higher achievement also in ethical terms. Everything we can share with others gives us in return a higher level of satisfaction. We can witness for ourselves the opposite reflection that can tell us where one stands, not on his own but in relation to friends, family and communities.

The 'moral aspect' of sharing life with less gifted individuals is a most valid one, as it touches base with the very existence of a human community. Only together, can we survive and the better we communicate, care for each other and act in a balanced way, the better quality of life we can uphold. To reiterate, the 'Simple Life' is found within the community in a sharing of lives with all levels of gifted individuals. It is very much an individual effort embarking on an isolated search in which responses to our existence are more likely to go missing.

We are not born to live our lives in isolation. From the first spark of life, we depend firstly on the support of our nearest fellow humans and we shouldn't abandon where we come from while growing into adulthood. To memorise, to act accordingly on hindsight and not just on foresight, has never been a human strength. Rather, we tend to forget things in life; this is where the all-encompassing human error starts. On the other hand, we can move away a little from an exclusive self-esteem and allow a broader circumspection with other human creatures. This is what makes us better humans on the way to a 'Simple Life'.

What would an updated example look like of 'sharing life with less gifted individuals'?

- Where would the world be today if we did not have an education system where formally educated people passed on knowledge sometimes by theory and sometimes by example? Students at an appropriate life stage take on board this knowledge to test in the real world to see whether or not it can build on their gifted talents. In that sense, education has the task to 'unlock' gifted as well as less gifted individuals to enable them to continue a life path of a broader insight. Ignorance on the other hand keeps people in isolation, depriving them of an informed say in their aspirations for quality of life.

    Every effort in education is justified as a worthwhile future investment as long as the individual is able to connect to said education. Everybody is gifted in the broadest sense, however to different degrees and in different fields. A lot of life experience is also required to find the key to reach less gifted individuals with their often less documented talents. Much depends here on a mutual will to meet on common ground.

- The 'social idea' as a whole is based on sharing life with less gifted individuals, which calls upon everybody to carry part of the load of others to sustain a better quality of life for more people and not selectively for a few chosen by discrimination.

With the emergence of the 'industrial revolution' at the end of the 19th century, the social idea progressed from the 'cradle', the need for social justice of that time ensuring the appropriate measures. However, during good times, social justice grew into a 'monster', mainly in the industrialised countries. At the start of the second millennium, it also turned into a powerful economic power of its own. A healthy economic balance between performance and social expectations will always demand a match of individual effort and received benefits. An imbalance, mainly in the area of receiving benefit, can trigger a downturn of all society's concerns.

- A (Finnish) fairytale (again author's own version), "Two butchers in hell," can teach us about sharing life with less gifted individuals : two brothers, one rich the other poor, were both butchers. The rich brother cherished evil senses whereas the poor one was filled with good-natured ones. As the poor brother couldn't do the slaughtering by himself, he usually gave his rich brother a helping hand. On one occasion, after a lot of arduous butchering work had been done during the course of one day, the poor brother became utterly exhausted. For all the work done, the self-appointed leader of the two brothers - the rich one - condescended to let his poor, less gifted brother have a lousy little sausage as a reward.

"Please give me another one for I worked the whole day alongside you," begged the less gifted, poorer brother.

"Here, have another one and go to hell with it; just leave me alone. I'm dog-tired, too," indignantly replied the rich brother.

After a good night's sleep, the less gifted brother indeed took the other brother's word seriously, setting out on the way to Hell. However, Hell being a fair distance away, it took the poor brother almost the entire next day to get there. On arrival, when daylight had turned already to dusk, the devils hadn't yet returned from work in the forest. There was only the grandma devil looking out of the window.

"Since when do humans walk this long distance to Hell? It's usually us, the devils that come to see humans."

"A good morning, dear grandma; how are you today?" bade the brother, continuing his welcome. "I didn't come here voluntarily; my brother sent me here with this sausage."

"Come closer and show me what you've got."

On closer inspection, the grandma devil retreated with the sausage into the hell-house, inviting the poor brother inside, too. A big fire filled the house with cosy warmth. Nobody else was around at the time so that the grandma devil found time to entertain the unexpected visitor. However, it was not for long as the time of the devils' homecoming drew closer. The brother ended up hiding under the grandma devil's bed just in time as the devil-pack stormed into the house.

"Dinner on the table; oh what a pain is our hunger," repeatedly shouted the entire pack of devils. "Wait, something smells like humans here," one of the devils shouted, looking suddenly around the room.

A steaming hot bowl, arriving on the table instantly diverted their attention.

"It's probably a leftover smell of a human who passed through earlier in the day," soothed the grandma devil.

Next morning after the devils had gone off to their daily work, collecting wood in the surrounding forests in order to maintain the hell-fire, the grandma devil took the secret visitor from under the bed, telling him, "Now you can confidently go back home. I give to you as my farewell one single devil's hair that I found on my pillow. Don't lose it; look after it!" So it was said and so it was done.

"God bless you, dear grandma," farewelled the good-natured, less gifted brother.

Back at his modest home, the poor brother watched in awe as the devil's hair developed into a huge haystack of pure gold. Suddenly, the poor, less gifted brother had become far richer than his rich, gifted brother had. He also gave proper employment to others in order to continue the butchering business without the need of his gifted, formerly richer brother.

Alas, green with envy to see the less gifted brother better off than himself, the gifted brother also set out to Hell with a big sausage of his own.

"What my dumb brother can do, I can do just as well."

Mockingly, without wishing a good morning, he arrived at Hell to see the grandma devil resting in the window again.

"What are you doing here, you old witch?" commenced the second brother.

"I'm waiting for your sausage."

"You won't have a bite on it with your rickety leftover teeth. The sausage is for the devils and I expect in return a golden haystack."

"Well you can have that, just come inside and wait here until the devils return home from their work in the forest." The gifted brother waited inside the house, sitting on a chair behind the door.

Later in the evening the devils burst into the house, yelling again, "Dinner on the table; oh what a pain hunger gives us!" Soon they sniffed however a foreign smell in the air. "It smells here of human flesh!"

"Behind the door is your prize catch waiting for you," indicated the grandma devil. The rich brother's fate was sealed. The devils wasted no time falling all over him, mercilessly shredding him into bits and pieces. From that moment on, the formerly poor, less gifted brother inherited also the wealth of his stingy, greedy brother.

This is how the world can sometimes work. The lesson learnt from this fairytale is still relevant today. Together, gifted and less gifted individuals can achieve more that points towards a 'Simple Life' than a few isolated individual attempts. The 'little things' make life worthwhile. He who surpasses them in a rush for greed will find himself disconnected from a shared life with others. Less gifted individuals are not here just to fill the lower ranks in societies. An understanding of them just needs individual attention to catch up with the rest of the community. It is a community responsibility to deliver this attention.

Inappropriate attention can work its way around us anyhow, with the difference that time only will tell us when we have 'missed the train' to carry us closer together. Then the 'bullet' bites back and more than just the less gifted ones find themselves in a shambles over a lack of shared attention.

However as we make history repeat itself, it has always been that 'the devil takes the hindmost' while the others seem to get away at least for the time being. Time is nature's equaliser, nothing is spared from it to render everything, and everybody equal finally. Short sightedness towards time makes us rush in front of everything and everybody only to bring us back to where we belong in another time, to nature.

CHAPTER 16

Living a Hermit's Life

What is the answer to the questions surrounding the living of life as a hermit? If there were straightforward answers, there would be no need to address the issue. On the contrary, most of us look at it with suspicion born out of uncertainty or ignorance. A hermit's life is a way out of this world that some do not want to live in all the time. Before looking for answers, a clear understanding of the issue can be useful.

A 'hermit' is someone who has retreated from a mainstream life into a secluded life of voluntary isolation. What is nature's answer to such a move? By looking into nature's diverse 'garden', we come across another species that lives the original hermit-like existence. The difference with this species is that it still shares life with its peers and does not completely isolate itself from its fellow creatures as its human counterpart does. Many of us have seen the quite unique hermit crab on sandy ocean beaches, rushing into their host shells for protection and digging deeper into moist sand to seek refuge from the flow of the sea onto a beach.

The hermit crab lives in a symbiotic relationship with the sea anemone. There is a mutual sharing of resources. The crab takes nutrients from the carrion on which it feeds, sharing this nutrition with the anemone, which in turn protects the crab in its shell by deterring predators by waving its tentacles. When growth forces the hermit crab to move to a bigger, empty shell housing, it will not leave behind its 'housemate'. Instead, it transfers the anemone to the new accommodation too.

The conclusion that can be drawn from this example is that nature provides the hermit crab with a mutual, useful coexistence with varying organisms. Humans, in their role as hermits however, have distanced themselves from any gainful coexistence with fellow creatures. It is here where the stark difference between human and animal 'hermits' is most obvious.

So what then are the motives behind humans living such a different hermit's life from that of nature's coexistent course? Renowned examples of human hermits are found in religious orders of monks and ascetics as well as those just living in seclusion. Despite the different constructs between human and nature's hermits, the human version does exist and has therefore to be respected. The task is to find out how human hermits' lives correspond with a 'Simple Life' and what their motives are.

Firstly, there are monks, who probably are known more by name than by first-hand experience in the Christian hemispheres of western industrialised countries. In Buddhist and Hindu cultures however, monks are a more common part of society. They are more integrated and are somewhat different from Christian monks who exercise humility and religious devotion in seclusion under the watchful eye of the church hierarchy.

Tradition has cemented many rules throughout history, which have advantaged one side of a society more than another. The Renaissance gave birth to many changes as we comprehend them. In such an 'awakening', it is irrelevant that monks have become a scarce commodity in our drive for progress that leaves everything falling behind eventually.

THE SIMPLE LIFE

People today increasingly seek answers about their existence away from the traditional established rules. Rather, they seek confirmation out of their world reality more often than with human fellow creatures. Undoubtedly, this is a shift towards self-determination with all its ups and downs as we all experience it. The more progress isolates us from nature's origins, the more we are bound to long for it, experiencing in retrospect the difficulties of reconnecting to something, which we've lost.

An earlier insight into the lives of monks is a reconnection in subjugating their lives to religious rules in order to retrace a path in the hope for a simpler or better life. In the case of a monk, his hermit-like life is actually run by an establishment, which distorts nature's course of survival. It is not the follower but the universally fittest in a constant process of adaptation, who is the survivor. For no other reason, a monk is buying his personal freedom in exchange for the uncertainties of a human existence. Here is the core motive of every hermit's life, whether it is a monk, an ascetic or an individual living in seclusion.

Ascetics are humans who have renounced material comforts to lead a life of austere self-discipline. It is a less exposed way of living under voluntarily reduced expectations. Sometimes however, ascetics resort to extreme expressions such as publicly demonstrated hunger strikes, the Indian fakir mastery of nail-bed resting, fire swallowing, and exerting hypnosis. A small part of this type of living in everyday life is like everything else; practised in moderation it can enhance daily life.

Some of the numerous forms of ascetic expressions bear further study. Despite being mainly a religious cultural tradition, ascetics encompass all physical and mental expressions of individuals in a world, which increasingly awakens towards the need of rebalancing life's imbalances. Efficiency as well as consistency are most difficult because rewinding such a process of imbalance is always more difficult than its unwinding.

Examples of ascetic expressions can be for instance: controlled eating habits, abstaining from alcohol/smoking, physical training, mental absorption, will training, suppression of selfishness, building on endurance, resilience, and last but not least compassion for others. All of these should be regarded as personal 'fine tuning' and not just magicians' tricks. It is simply a matter of setting individual goals or following others' examples with increased personal efforts rather than trying with inadequate backup. In that sense, personal ascetics can become a positive force in a hermit's life as long as they do not cause a severing of ties with society's mainstream. If nothing is left to feed back into society, a hermit's life has moved into an isolation out of which neither party, the individual nor the community, will reap real benefits.

A hermit's life in total seclusion still needs to be addressed. People retreat from life challenges into seclusion for many reasons most of which are a response to a personality conflict or disorder with other people. The decision then is often taken to move away from what cannot either be fully comprehended and therefore satisfactorily managed.

People matching this description range from the traditional dropouts, failures, or brooders right through to the serious contenders. They all have in common a lifestyle, which they think, saves them from unnecessary conflict with other people. In fact, people living in this type of seclusion often are not commonly visible within the fabric of society, thereby receiving little if any attention from the public.

To be such a reclusive can be confusing to the extent that neither the individual nor the public can clearly identify any more who is to blame for this situation. An impasse can then become responsible for a deepening division between the hermit and the public. To rejoin the discussion through mutual understanding becomes a complex task for either side. Like everything else in life, the path to a hermit-like life usually starts with little steps, which in the early stages can look insignificant but constitutes enough to trigger a chain reaction leading to total seclusion.

Children at various developmental stages for instance like to revolt against parental guidance. Such early conflict can lead to a distancing of relations, especially if both sides have not found common ground. The elder and wiser should be able to give enough room for the younger to find their own place in a community. In any case, the blame game never helps when trying to solve anything with regard to human relations.

Once a defeat, a rejection or even a misunderstanding has been left unattended, a path away from a majority understanding has been established. Continued failure to connect or compromise is a sure pathway to a life of seclusion, a hermit's life. Once having arrived there, a person usually feels misunderstood in the first place, which intensifies the seclusion. Misfortune or tragedy can also lead individuals into seclusion if a process of reconciliation with losses is never addressed. First signs of a breakdown in communication show up in close relations with family and friends when an understanding withers away mostly for a lack of dealing with quite minor issues.

Not all is bad however with the life of a hermit. Some individuals get lost in seclusion while others can build strength from this position. All depends on which side of the seclusion equation, useful or less useful, the hermit lies. It is not necessary to step far from accustomed life to meet somebody living the hermit's life. All that is needed is close observation.

In the midst of a crowd or in 'residential silos', it is easy to spot those living the life of a hermit. Most individuals don't know each other, let alone know each other's names, which is the manifestation of a mass society, which reduces individual interplay. If we were to investigate further, it would probably show that, in reality, everybody carries a load of problems, some more, some less conveniently hidden. Only then a more representative, more widely acceptable personal image can 'steal the show'.

A discrepancy between supporting loaded, unfinished personal problems and performing a 'show' can determine the position in a community an individual can hold. More 'unfinished business' tends to prove decisive, leading to a move towards a reclusive life even in the midst of fellow citizens. If an individual doesn't have a release valve to diminish their personal insecurities then this leads to further insecurities of all dimensions.

To achieve this 'release valve', a person who has become stuck in a roundabout life, simply needs to follow the common sense path of speaking to others in an unbiased manner. If such a move remains blocked, not enough efforts at reconciliation have been put forward and further immersion into seclusion results. This amounts to an increased withdrawal from mainstream society. Such a move can then become detrimental to an individual's well-being.

On the other hand, individuals can make their own decisions either to live a hermit's life or they can be driven by circumstances into it. Some individuals might seek liberation from 'unfinished business pressure' in order to find a way of dealing with it through reduced expectations. Then, through individual efforts, they can rebuild more of a stand in the society, which they then comprehend better. Eventually they will emerge stronger and make their way back into the mainstream world.

To illustrate the differences in typical hermit lifestyles, some practical illustrations can assist. There are two types of hermits that have left the everyday community. One is the complete isolate and the other lives very close to us.

A young man has just decided he has had enough of all the daily hassle, obligations, and pressure to please so many others around him. "Why not leaving this curse of noisy city life, this crazy beehive and move into the nearby forests which are an oasis of peace? I'm sure a peaceful life can be found there."

Such were the young man's thoughts, not only for moments of each day but repeatedly throughout the long, cold winter months until finally spring arrived. Keeping the plan firmly to himself, Michael took off into the nearby forest so that nobody knew of his whereabouts. Deep inside the dense fir-tree canopy where no forest path intruded, Michael started collecting fallen branches. He found them under the less common deciduous trees and laid them out in the air between four evenly spaced tree trunks, which formed the outline of a room. Thin willow-twigs from the surrounding undergrowth served well to hold the roof firmly on to the tree trunks at a height, which allowed Michael to move around upright inside.

More selected branches were placed first vertically, evenly spaced in the surrounding walls and braided horizontally from bottom to top with other branches. In addition to filling all open spaces with new foliage shoots and fern leaves, two openings were left: a door and a window. During that day, time was completely forgotten. Sunset announced the end of the day, making Michael realise that on one hand, a good day's toil had been done but much more had been left unfinished.

Having become too tired to look around for food, Michael instantly fell asleep in his forest home. An undisturbed night's sleep gave Michael the energy to start another day. Everything here remained silent except nature's birdsong overtures. No human interference ensured that Michael could spend another day exactly as he chose. Even his cautious footsteps on the forest floor sent rustling noises from cracking fallen leafs and little branches into the still air between the silently upward pointing tree columns.

Water was first on Michael's mind, then food for his rumbling stomach. Patience, well-honed observation and adaptation plus that important bit of good luck helped Michael tackle these first hurdles. He found water in a nearby forest run-off; food was more difficult. Hunger and lean times demanded Michael's quick inventiveness. Before trying to trap a hare or capture a bird high in the forest canopy, he rather collected from the ground stinging nettles, dandelions, freshly dug chanterelle, and cut-up tree bark and cooked these in an abandoned tin over a fireplace between set rocks. All this had to satisfy Michael for the time being.

The challenge of which stick could deliver the necessary spark onto dry grass when twisted in a small rock cavity had become a big problem. Once Michael had managed to start a fire for cooking, the next step became to keep the ashes at least glowing so he didn't have to go through the whole fire-starting procedure again. Unlike before, there was nobody around to help him solve the problem. Everything now had become his sole responsibility.

Here in the seclusion of the forest, no clock measured the time; everything demanded its own time. Without alternatives, any 'need for speed' was irrelevant. Everything Michael needed he had to learn to provide for himself from what occurred naturally around him. Already, after just one day, the message had sunk in. If you want to go it alone, it demands exceptional personal efforts. From here on, it was up to Michael to prove himself.

The question could arise whether or not it might be useful to turn back the clock of evolution in order to engage ourselves as far back as the Stone Age in terms of developmental stages. This cannot be the answer for a 'Simple Life' either because the efforts in retracing the paths of where we came from are always disproportionate to temporary inconveniences. Therefore, it didn't come as a surprise that Michael found, sooner rather than later, a way back into a life shared with others. Michael's attempt at a hermit's life had been a case of voluntary decisions.

But how about when decisions are enforced on someone from outside such as during war times or in the aftermath of war? I still remember the early years after World War II. As a child, not having much comparison yet in an inexperienced life, everything did appear more like irreversible fact. This was not so much the case for the majority of adults who had seen better times.

Already in the aftermath of World War I, many people throughout war-battered Europe made decisions to move to other parts of the world in the hope of finding a more peaceful life. Some of them had chosen to turn their back on civilization and search for a new life somewhere else. When making a decision to move from what was virtually the cradle of European culture and civilization into a life in the Brazilian 'Mato Grosso', (jungle), one must have strong motives. Much courage was also needed to pursue a contentious life even if it was to take more time than could have been initially anticipated.

In one case, it was Alexander joined by his wife Erika and their son, holding their own territory and living a real hermit's life in the jungle. During the first years, almost nothing came their way, which they couldn't tackle. At first, they had to clear a living area in the midst of dense rainforest vegetation, cultivating soil for growing beans, cassava (manioc), taro, sweet potato and much more of what the jungle held. A solid house was built out of river rocks and after the first essential needs had been met for survival, their individual interests gained momentum through exploring and documenting nature in its kingdom, including the tropical rain forests.

Developing and writing a language to communicate across the whole world was their next priority. 'Esperanto' (the hopeful) was the language that proved popular with Erika Linz, the wife of Alexander. It was the first constructive language, which developed out of mainly Roman and Anglo-Saxon lingual sources, aimed to reach and connect people across the world. The language was originally established by the Polish linguistics Doctor Ludwig Zamenhof around 1887. The convention of the other languages remained dominant however, in particular English which superseded Esperanto in its universally intended objectives.

Mind power had created here in the jungle a hermit's life with a completely new life dimension, allowing the eruption of small individual life cells into the world through remaining steadfast in the ties with nature. Yet the tide of fate turned against Alexander, who in later life succumbed to frail health; his son fell victim to a snakebite and wife Erika, trapped in seclusion, turned back to her previous life from which she had escaped 60 years earlier. 'What goes up has also to come down again'. Does fate render everything and everybody equal so that nobody can hold sway for too long? During the course of a life, can we really talk of 'failure', or is it simply 'repatriation' to something more sustainable in nature's terms?

The 'Simple Life' in this case was not a 'contract' of a lifetime. Like everything else, the 'Simple Life' is a personal achievement, which remains subjugated to the ups and downs of everyday issues. Sometimes we have to stay watchful in order not to miss out on it as we can never know for sure when we've peaked and found the 'Simple Life'. Only the opposite of our expectations can tell us whether life is travelling uphill or downhill. It is best not to miss that particular 'train' and to be content with every day of our life, enjoying the uphill journey as it happens and not trying to force the issue of pursuit of the 'Simple Life'.

There is another slant to living a hermit's life which exists in close proximity to us in our highly industrialised world and which will demand our attention at some stage. Increasingly it is the elderly who are living hermit-like lives often in the midst of a pulsing community life around them. Progress demands more and more attention from those driving the progress spiral. As a result, people outside the mainstream often find themselves pushed aside, more or less forgotten in the ever-escalating push for increased consumerism. Sometimes, the elderly are regarded as having done their duty, having passed their 'use by date' and are left behind in their own little hermit lives.

An example of this was Aunty Lotte as she was known in town. For over 40 years, she had delivered the newspaper around town. When her aged legs couldn't carry her any more over the daily distance of the labyrinth of streets in old Heidelberg, her service was cancelled with the stroke of a pen for nothing more than economic considerations. A tailored pension helped Aunty Lotte retire and consequently she now had to lead a life cut off from the many people she used to see. No more could she engage in the so important interpersonal chats while delivering the newspaper.

Time meanwhile meant her previous customers forgot about her because more pressing issues had besieged their minds. Was there somebody specific to blame for the situation Aunty Lotte found herself in all of a sudden? Probably nobody ever asked this question anyway, because the general social system was put in charge of what was left behind. Here, words too cannot speak for action; they can help send somebody into detrimental isolation if mutual understanding is not given appropriate attention. Aunty Lotte in fact, spent the rest of her life becoming increasingly abandoned by her fellow citizens because everybody was so preoccupied with their own lives.

To express compassion with words is regarded as a virtue but it often falls short of the more important action, which should follow. When a light at the end of the tunnel did appear for Aunty Lotte, it was not for long because with time, people's lives moved in different directions, hardly remaining steadfast in one place any more. The world had kept moving on and the same people with whom she had previously shared her life banished Aunty Lotte to leading the life of a hermit.

Not everybody can stand up on his own and follow the everyday leaders in order to be heard. It is especially difficult for the vulnerable within a society: the little, the aged, the sick and the disadvantaged. Such a deprived life cannot be regarded as a 'Simple Life' because the dialogue has gone missing between fellow humans who are forced to find an escape in other outlets such as nature, pets, and gardening - environments that have been left largely unchanged.

My own family experienced firsthand the loneliness in which Aunty Lotte found herself. For a short time, our presence became a light in her life but soon our own conditions were demanding that we move on in our lives just like everybody else did. We did our best to bridge the gap of communication while we could but it was sad to hear Aunty Lotte say, "When you leave, I've nobody anymore and might as well turn on the gas tap." All I can say is that I hope she didn't do it.

My family moved to live and work in South Africa at that time and with the distance between us, we lost contact with Aunty Lotte. However, it needs to be said that nobody can take complete responsibility for other people's lives, especially if they choose not to put in an effort of their own to keep their social circle open. Life has to carry on even under the most difficult conditions. Aunty Lotte's hermit period could not classify as a 'Simple Life' because there was too much pain and negativity in that period of her life. This left her vulnerable and living in a virtual prison with no escape obvious to her.

Not all hermits' lives are necessarily bad though. An example of this could be a person who lives in the community of a township that could be anywhere in the developed part of the world today. The difference here however is that the individual has not turned, nor been turned physically away from the mainstream society. Individual decisions coupled with outside pressures can also move a strong person into leading a hermit's life. Here, the emphasis is on a strong inner-person who seeks time in seclusion in order to work out an individual understanding of a quality life away from the often-confusing diversity of mainstream society. They are the people living a more private life than the majority in a neighbourhood usually does.

A number of reasons can lead to living in the seclusion of a hermit: experiences which on a personal level are difficult in some way or other: distress with other people, sickness, opposition to mainstream society or voluntary retreat from a hurried and stressful life – in fact, anything can lead to the positive aspects of living of a hermit's life. This can be resting, engaging in physical exercise geared to an individual level i.e. gentle but regular walking and swimming, exploring the gardener's life, reading books, listening and/or practising music, simply taking the time to think more deeply about life issues.

Everything an individual manages by and large for himself, without the need of direct support from others, can be a good way to raise one's own awareness and skills. However, a few like-minded individuals sharing their independence can also be regarded as one of the most positive variations on living the life of a hermit. On the other hand, negative attitudes, which produce only negative outcomes, can haunt the individual hermit's life. Negative is here regarded as everything, which does not further a better, simpler life.

A down-to-earth tale can demonstrate what is considered the 'right' or 'wrong' aspects of a hermit's life: a peasant has worked a lifetime – every day from early morning until late evening - on the farm he took over from his parents. He worked every day of the week including weekends. The farm's livestock of pigs, cattle and horses did not 'know' about time off, consistently demanding every day to be fed and looked after. The peasant therefore had no choice but to be up and working every day too.

His two sons had completed the minimum local school requirements with little enthusiasm. They should have followed in their father's footsteps and helped to work the farm. One of the sons set to work on the difficult task of daily farm work whereas the other one idled around, no matter what kind of work it was. One day the father became sick of watching his lazy son and wracked his brain about what to do with him. Inwardly, he couldn't but think that eventually the two sons would quarrel with each other, not over work but over who will have the better slice of the farm. Not losing his cool over such an uncertain future, the peasant circumvented the decision by sending both sons out into the world to learn to stand on their own before claiming improperly what he and his ancestors had built.

The hard-working son became the first to understand the father's decision and set off not too far away from the parents' farm. Every so often, he paid them a visit to keep in touch even if it was just for a short time occasionally. On his part, the hard-working son couldn't see any harm in the decision that his father had made. The other brother however had become angry at the father's decision, swearing never to return home. Rather, he would leave the 'old man' high and dry instead of bending to his rule.

Again, the old blame-game meant that the lazy son always called others to account for shortcomings in his own expectations. He looked for all sorts of excuses for not finding a more decent roof over his head away from home. Why did nobody want to give him money for work? It probably had something to do with his neglected appearance of untidy shoes, dirty clothes, and long unkempt hair, which made it obvious to others that work, wasn't his primary concern. Hope of a better life faded by the day, steering the lazy brother into the seclusion of a negative hermit-like existence. In his eyes, others were to blame for the little that people still gave him despite his unpleasant attitude.

The diligent brother not only looked after his own life but also never abandoned a closeness with his parents or his brother. Yet he found time enough to look after his own life, which from the start moved him into a promising direction. While looking for work in the nearby town bakery, he had put on his best clothes, asking for whatever work there was. The baker's wife straightaway put him into work clothes, giving him the first taste of what she understood about work.

The diligent brother gave his best efforts and within hours received appreciation from the baker. It also secured for him not only work but also full board and lodging. After work, the lad was happy enough learning to lead his own life by staying put in his room instead of spending his hard-earned money in other people's places. This spare time, he realised, was best used paying attention to what he enjoyed doing in addition to his work: reading and learning more and keeping in touch with other people, all of which added to a slow but healthy growth in his new life.

If in life we don't do something, it's hardly realistic to expect other people to do it for us; life couldn't work that way. Because of the diligent brother's concern also for others, he never lost the big picture of caring about the wellbeing of his close relations. Firmly and with convincing strength, he could move from his position of being partly entrenched in a hermit's life, out to meet others without compromising his own objectives.

And so with time, he did see his brother and parents on their farm on more regular terms. The parents found themselves in somewhat of a hermit's life of their own because the bulk of work on the farm only diminished their lives, overtaxing them by and large. The diligent son, enjoying the positive side of life, was able to respond reasonably to the needs of his parents who had found themselves more in the negative territory of a life.

The diligent brother became the one to break the silence in the family again, once more engaging everybody in dialogue. What had become distant moved closer through a dialogue over time. The successful brother moved back onto the parents' farm, helping them once more. Not long after, the ice melted somewhat and the father called on the down-and-out-son. In repeatedly joint efforts, the whole family found unity again. Everybody had tested the waters, learnt useful lessons and could return to a common place. As long as one side at least maintained a positive outlook on life, all was well. It is easy to see how a hermit's life can become a road sign to a 'Simple Life' if it does not lead to a dead end road through the long-term absence of dialogue with others.

A Finnish fairytale can further demonstrate the pros and cons of a hermit's life: once upon a time, three beautiful sisters lived in the north of the world where in the middle of summer the sun still shines on the horizon even in the middle of the night. Around a bonfire, people usually gathered not only to celebrate joyful the occasion but also to give the magic of the moment over to listening to individual wishes for a better life.

The three sisters, amongst others, told each other their most secret wishes. One wished to become the wife of the King's butler, the second of his chef and the third wanted the King's son for her husband. What all three sisters didn't realise was that the King's son had mixed within the gathering and heard the three sisters' wishes. He responded openly to them, "All three of you are so beautiful that your sincere wishes should not go unanswered. I'm granting all three wishes in person."

The sister who the King's son picked for his wife was overwhelmed with joy. The other two sisters, who all of a sudden considered their choice less noble, were not so thrilled. Not long after, the two sisters hammered out a sinister plan. When the King's son was away on a foreign battlefield, his wife gave birth to their first son. The two sisters came to assist but used the absence of the King's son to put their sinister plan in place. They exchanged the baby boy with an ugly puppy dog. Upon seeing the ugly 'child', everybody in the Kingdom dismissed the new Queen's qualification to deliver the line of succession to the Throne.

When, after a few more years, this incident had repeated itself twice, the Queen was put into seclusion in a solid, closed fortress tower. She had to survive solely on bread and water to repent for how she had belittled the Royal reputation. The Queen however, never gave up hope that the truth would one day get her out of her miserable hermit's life. What nobody else, except the two deceitful sisters knew, was the way they had made the three newborn babies disappear.

It was the King's gardener who, just by accident, picked the sorry looking, floating bundles out of the passing river and, as he had no children, raised all three with lots of care and love, as his own. When grown up, they all three helped in the garden. They too heard that the Queen was locked away for many years in a cold, dark tower of the Palace. Like every other decent person, they too felt compassion for such a wrecked human fate.

Meanwhile the unjustly incarcerated Queen continued incessantly to hope, planning for her life once out of this imprisonment. The gardener had a repeated dream that the only way to get the Queen out of her prison was by a pilgrimage of each of the children to the Palace. Only children would have the magic power to free a mother from unjust imprisonment. The dream also told the gardener how to go about it: go and face the direction of the prison tower but do not look behind or you'll become transformed into stone.

The boy of the three children was the first to go, failing however in following the rule not to become confused with what happened behind him, no matter what. The boy and one of his sisters who followed could not refrain from looking behind to listen to the rumours and noises of the others. The third sister however, saw this and plugged her ears in order not to hear anything that reached her from behind. She made it to the tower and saw for the first time a hopeful, strong, unbroken Queen.

Nobody could deny the resemblance of mother and child. This happy reunion also brought back to life the stone-transformed brother and sister. The King then ordered the Queen's two guilty sisters to be locked away into the Palace tower so that they could think long and hard of what they had personally done to his family and the whole Kingdom.

A hermit's life can be especially useful through its seclusion, in reminding us of our strength of mind in tackling life from this side. Sometimes we have to retreat from the mainstream in order to build our individual strength so that we regain the necessary confidence in a stand with others. To be a 'Jack of all trades' with others can be quite popular on one side, but to remain solely on that side can lead to personal neglect and unavoidably to losses.

The right balance is then again the answer. A life that includes time as a hermit when individual events demand it can still be fruitful. We need to read these signs for our own good because this is where everything starts in a community. A contentious balance between want and need can make people retreat to the refuge of a hermit's life, even if it is only temporarily.

CHAPTER 17

Following the Life of a 'Jack of All Trades'

Most people would have both a positive and a negative perception of a 'Jack of all trades'. Their understanding would depend on the occasion in which they find themselves in terms of equal opportunities. One person might be struggling with his/her bit to perform a single limited task while somebody else can appear at times to be doing everything effortlessly. If this other person performs visibly, one feels inclined to give the venture a stamp of high approval. It is important though that the venture is not just a façade with little foundation. Generally, this would not stand up to close scrutiny.

How do we recognise the positive or negative side of a 'Jack of all trades' and how could it affect a 'Simple Life'? Firstly, let us shed some light on the positive side. A fence line needs to be renewed along a sheep property in the Outback. New wooden poles are set first at regular distances of five metres to allow five strips of barbwire to be fixed at equal spaces. Modern technology can help today by diminishing some of the hard work that previous hand digging operations demanded from its operators. A two-stroke driven spiral drill operates more easily unless the ground is infested with rocks. A strong man can hold the drill firmly for the required twist of the handles.

The heat of the sun in such places during the day is debilitating, which makes the job only more draining. No technology is failure-proof and so it is with the post-hole digging machine. If it stops operating for no apparent reason, the man on the handles is left to do what is in his power to continue with the job. A motor mechanic is not an option because the workshop of a mechanic is not on hand. Calmly, the operator looks thoroughly at various parts of the equipment.

Our operator is not a motor mechanic but has been putting up fences for many years and has learnt to fix many problems simply because no alternative options were on hand. Necessity has always driven his mind for the solution to a problem. When a mechanic is required, our post-hole digger manages to find the mechanical solution, albeit often outside the traditional method. It might be a 'magical' cleaning, a knock here and there, bypassing this with that, wire helping to replace a lost screw and much more of what real ingenuity can bring to the problem. The relentless heat begs a speedy fix as time dragging on only makes matters worse.

At the end, the engine prevails with a 'cough' and the operational pause finally roars into life again. The components of the drill-spiral have also been cleaned of a heavy burr build up and resharpened with a simple file. A no-rush principle helped secure a positive outcome, also allowing our operator to take a break with a deep, long draught from the contents of the 'esky'. Our 'Jack of all trades' met success in the middle of nowhere because of wanting to complete the fencing work, which asked for many more stopgap solutions.

Without detailing further examples of a positive understanding of the 'Jack of all trades', people can have this experience by stepping outside of daily routines into a less comfortable environment. People will soon realise that without readily accessible professional solutions, one has to find simple solutions from which positive outcomes can be achieved. Ingenuity, perseverance, calm, creativity, 'stick-to-it-ness', and having a sense for small details; these are all ingredients of a positive understanding of the 'Jack of all trades'.

Education can help with getting back to the basics but alone, it cannot do much if it hasn't been put to the test in practical situations. It is important that a person has the ability to adapt by focussing on a practical solution rather than the focus being on a missed education. A 'Jack of all trades' can be found in all areas of life, no matter how small they might be. Even a clerk in an established office-environment, which is supposed to run in an organised fashion with everything on hand, will be called upon by others to find that missing link between organisation and its shortcomings.

What causes the perception of a 'Jack of all trades' to be negative? Surprisingly, the vernacular has more to say on the negative side than the positive. People verbalise this negativity in phrases such as: 'Jack of all trades, master of none', 'Every Jack has his Jill, if one won't, the other will' and 'All work and no play makes Jack a dull boy'.

The first adage seems to caution us to be wary of the person who knows a little about many different things. We all deal daily with tasks which are given to us or that we've set ourselves. Most of the time we struggle enough with one task and look suspiciously at somebody who showily handles more than one task. However, by looking more closely into this situation, it becomes evident that only one task at a time can be dealt with successfully before another one is taken on. 'Jack' can either lose track in pursuing systematic tasks or solve comprehensively coherent tasks. It is here that Jack receives the label of 'positive' or 'negative'.

If a practical individual comes face to face with a practical 'misfit', the latter usually has difficulties in understanding the other side, which can lead to a disparagement born out of ignorance. In fact, a master emerges only when there is a restriction to one task at a time. The individual who takes on more than one task at a time is likely to become master of none, overpowered by time and the sheer load of work, resulting in stress. Complexity in a task is best dealt with by a breaking-down of the job into smaller tasks. Then one can tackle one task at a time by reviewing priorities each time one small task has been eliminated satisfactorily. Everything else makes 'Jack', master of no trade.

The second maxim, 'Every Jack has his Jill, if one won't, the other will' tends to paint 'Jack' as unpredictable even unreliable. Everything in life goes round; there will always be another 'Jack' or 'Jill' to tackle a task. It is a matter of whether or not the task will outmanoeuvre one Jack or permeate to other Jacks in a stronger team formation in which Jack is given a better chance through cooperation. Here, 'more strings to a bow', can help 'Jack' but it is not a *fait accompli* as the genuine individual resolve can still hang in limbo.

It is said with good reason that 'many cooks can spoil the soup' and 'the spice to the soup only comes from one cook'. How many times have we seen a community task watered down to something that is very different from the original concept? As long as we can move on, it will get us somewhere, even if it is along an unpredictable route. Nature is here calling upon us by giving priority to the accidental outcome ahead of our planned undertakings. He who challenges nature, either knowingly or ignorantly, will again rely upon nature's reasoning, regardless of a 'Jack' or not. Everything is on the move towards a place where we are banished to the role of an observer. Good observing has always helped find the better solution. Here emerges another 'Jack' key with a good observation for details.

'All work and no play' sees our 'Jack of all trades' turning into a dull boy judged by his ability to handle a task either with stress or in comfort. When the crucial play aspect goes missing in what we do, joy becomes a distant memory. As a child, we learnt best through play and should not forget this when moving into adulthood. Play in any learning situation can help give us a balanced performance. It can ensure we stay open to learning in an unbiased way from a wider option platform. On the other hand, the one who is absorbed with a task to the point of isolation is 'Jack' turning into a dull boy. Most people around 'Jack' would not understand the essence of a task.

'Going it alone' can eventually result in a speedy facility but cannot unambiguously exclude the possibility of missing crucial stages on the way. On the other hand, one has to abandon isolation and allow others to participate. These other participants can scrutinise the individual's efforts with support and timely criticism. 'Going it alone' can result in a quick but rarely permanent success making 'Jack' the dull boy.

Inevitably, the question remains: how much does a 'Jack of all trades' serve the 'Simple Life'? The answer lies in another axiom: 'If a job is worth doing, it's worth doing well.' A challenge for Jack here becomes doing the right thing for Jack, the job and for others, which ultimately makes him 'Jack of all trades.' To do the right thing for others, let alone for everybody, is indeed difficult enough on its own. The only way Jack can maintain his reputation when performing a complex task is to not do too little or too much, finding instead the right balance without losing a necessary circumspection for other surrounding issues. Then a 'Simple Life' is given more of a chance to not become displaced through performance pressure.

Time also plays a vital role in compensating for shortcomings, which under pressure can easily become overlooked. Difficulties, the opposition to a 'Simple Life', establish themselves from a too close perspective rather than from a distance, because the latter allows time for better judgement.

Our 'Jack of all trades' epigram can be illustrated by a fairytale: once upon a time, there was a father and mother with a son who had just finished at the local basic school. At the age of fourteen, the parents wanted their son to learn a trade, which they believed would enable him in the coming years to lead a more independent life than they had enjoyed.

The shoemaker in the neighbourhood became the first choice because he had known the boy's parents all his life. In addition, the proximity of the shoemaker's shop to their home made everything so much easier. The difficulties of school life all of a sudden disappeared, so that the son progressed quickly under the master's guidance. Soon the son could do all the work related to shoemaking by himself. He could repair as well as make new shoes of all styles and applications.

"What can I learn next?" the son asked his parents, who were not prepared for this question or for even thinking about such a possibility. In their past, youth were contented enough if they were offered a single trade, no matter what it was. An uneasy feeling dogged the parents as they considered the unsettled life they thought their son was starting. They wanted stability and security for him.

Yet the son made up his own mind, beginning practical instruction lessons with a blacksmith. When the son had completed and mastered all aspects of the blacksmith's trade, he again looked for something else. Everything the son learnt, he practised to perfection in next to no time. The parents received only good reports but could not get used to their son's idea of constantly moving on. Window and mirror making were also included in the son's learning curve.

One day when the son paid his parents a visit, the issue of his future was raised in a heated discussion. "What do you want? All your learning gets you nowhere if you don't settle for one trade. Don't tell us that you want to make another move and if so, what will it be this time?"

"I had a dream the other night in which I wanted to learn the language of the birds and this is now what I intend to do."

"You must have lost your senses by the way you talk to us. Who the hell wants to learn such a stupid thing?"

"Don't you worry; the birds also told me in the dream that I'll become wealthy and my parents will have the privilege of serving my morning cup of coffee to me in bed."

"You are not only out of your senses but crazy, and on top of that an impudent son who shows no respect to his poor parents anymore. We don't want to see you like this; from now on you are on your own!"

"I promise to show you due respect in the not too distant future."

Off went the son into the meadows that surrounded the small hometown before dense forest took over. He was looking for the oak tree, which housed in his dream whole flocks of birds. Finding an old growth tree standing free in the green grass fields was an easy task. Firstly, only few birds perched hidden in the monstrous branch crown of the tree. Not long after the son haltingly mimicked bird sounds, more birds flocked to the tree, seemingly from nowhere and joined in with the singing and bird talking. The son had no trouble picking up the bird 'language' and soon was proud of his latest achievement.

Meanwhile, the King had been looking around in his country for somebody who could replace one of his golden shoes, which had disappeared under strange circumstances. The King announced that whoever could make the missing shoe identical to the existing one, would be rewarded with as much gold as he/she can take into one hand. The son answered the call in person and had to listen carefully to the conditions.

"If you make a good job, you'll earn gold; but if you fail, you'll be jailed." The King wouldn't accept any other quality except that of his existing shoe. Even in the given time of one day, the son presented the finished shoe to perfection and was going to receive the golden coins when the King asked the son for another favour. "Can you make me a standing mirror in a wooden frame, lined with diamonds which I'll supply you?"

Needing little time for consideration, the son immediately started and again, sooner than the King could expect, the job was finished. When the mirror arrived for the King's critical inspection, he had to say, "To tell the truth, you are an outstanding tradesman but what I also want to know is whether you are wise. To prove this, I entrust you with my deepest secret. My wife, the Queen, had a baby daughter but I have never seen our baby. If you were to find out about my daughter and what has happened to her, you'll have a carefree, luxurious life in the castle for the rest of your life."

The son agreed to the task and thoroughly pondered his dream about the mighty tree with the birds. To do so, he returned to the tree welcomed by noisy bird chatter. Here, the son told the birds what the King had asked him to find out. Without hesitation, the birds told him that a couple of years ago the baby girl of the King had been buried under the tree early in the morning. Since then, the tree had begun to show signs of sickness.

When this message reached the King, he shook his head in disbelief. "I will have the tree removed, but if you are wrong, you will face my prison for deliberately misleading the King."

The tree was then cut down and while digging under the tree trunk, the remains of the baby girl were indeed discovered. On first hearing about it and then confirming this with an inspection, the King himself brought his wife to justice by locking her in a deep, dark tower prison. He then redeemed his promise to the skilled and wise son to live from now on side by side with the King in a luxurious and unburdened life.

The son's parents were so happy to see him succeed so nobly that they forgot all about the past discords and happily agreed to live close by with their son in the castle and truly serve the morning cup of coffee to their famous son while he was still in bed.

What makes a 'Jack of all trades' is the practical use of what he/she has learnt. A link to the 'Simple Life' is demonstrated by a restriction to details from whence a master emerges without the unwelcome stress load of unfinished business.

CHAPTER 18

Helping Other People

'Help has no pay, but many rewards.' This is the fundamental difference between everything that we do. If it isn't helping, it indulges in money and money soils everything. Money is the goal towards which everything pushes. Any wonder that 'help' is written in such small letters in so many people's consciousness. However, the ones who do help stand out in this mass of money pushers.

How is it then that the 'help' gene appears in some lives and not in others? It is also said, 'every little bit helps' which indicates that 'help' finds its field of action predominantly with the endless little things of our lives. Because being little and almost confusing in their numbers, those small but very influential needs are the very foci of our lives. The one who wants to give a helping hand first has to recognise the almost insignificant aspects among the significantly larger and more demanding issues.

Spontaneous help is the best type of help. It does eventually include unexpected surprises for the one who is in need of help. Whether help is needed in crowded inner-city places or in secluded privacy, spontaneous help has the universal distinction of bringing a surprise into the life of the recipient.

For instance, in a main arterial of an inner city, a shop is receiving a facelift. A number of contract workers put the final touch on the façade of the building. Like everything else in today's world, time is running out for the job completion so that short cuts are used to try to make up some time. Inevitably, problems sneak in. During a typically rushed afternoon, a scaffolding plank is picked up from the ground. One end of it lags behind because of its weight so that the plank is halfway into the scaffolding when it gets stuck. At that very moment, the owner of the shop happens to inspect progress of the renovation work. He himself doesn't muck around but lends a hand straight away and off goes the plank, successfully slotted into the scaffolding gap. The little dirt on his hand from the plank doesn't overly worry him; the main thing is that the job is done with that crucial little bit of help from the owner.

"You were just in time and a great help. Thank you very much. We can now continue doing our best to give your shop a great new look and finish the job today, come what may," assures the job supervisor. Not only was the job secured with this little bit of help, but encouragement for completion of the job was renewed. It also ensured a two-way appreciation as a reward between supervisor and shop owner. Such a small intervention did so much.

An unselfish willingness to help sees many individuals perform great acts of heroism. A head-on collision between two cars occurred on a winding road far from any city-based emergency services. The first car arriving at the scene stopped at a safe distance and the driver grabbed the fire extinguisher from his car and hurried into the intense inferno, which already engulfed parts of the wreckage. When the rescuer saw passengers trapped in the wreckage, he pulled one person out through the broken rear window. The heat became so intense that the rescuer would have become a victim if he had not retreated in time from the scene. The realities of such incidents are often recorded in the news reporting. 'After pulling at least one passenger out of the burning wreckage of a two-car road accident, the rescuer himself was knocked down by a passing car which was speeding and was fatally injured.' Here the helper focussed so strongly on getting others out of danger that his own safety became his secondary concern.

This shows a 'noble character' which usually goes back a long way in the life of an individual. Typically, it starts in early childhood with parental support for ethical behaviour. Then, many years of individual experiences helps form a humble self-esteem coupled with strong views towards not only fellow humans but towards living forms as a whole. Even when caught in the middle, unconditional help offered to others remains one of humankind's highest achievements.

However, everything, including instances of selfless help, turns controversial with time. The result might be controversial in which one outcome is likely to be tragic while another outcome embarks on a said superior attitude in life. Real nobility in action is the best anybody can expect in life. Shirkers on the other hand bring out only cowardice, which is anything but noble. Nobility registers with our fellow creatures more profoundly and permanently than weighing up the pros and cons of help for individual benefit.

Examples of selfless help are found in all walks of life. In Australia, two of the most recognised are surf lifesavers and animal rescue. Saving lives along the vast, naturally beautiful but also dangerous coastline of Australia is something we often take for granted, but lifesavers have been performing this task for many years. They are well established on beaches of densely populated areas where people seek freedom from the demands of city-life. Our enjoyment of our beautiful beaches in Australia can be marred by many dangers - from strong ocean currents, rips, mighty waves of the oceans, dangerous sea-creatures to the intense sun radiation, which causes skin cancer.

In such an environment of riotous leisure time, the young, fit, strong swimmers are stationed along sections of particularly frequented beaches, boats anchored in the shallow surf ready for the rescue of wayward swimmers and surfers. The unpredictable coastal waters ensure the lifesavers have plenty to do. Thanks to their presence and supportive measures in the water, they have saved many lives. Like buoys marking a safe distance for swimmers, nets destined to keep out mainly shark predators and the striking gold and red flags, all have helped in the saving of lives, which daily face the dangers of the sea.

Lifesavers are constantly trained in their clubs for quick, strong responses to a rescue call. They often risk their own lives in hazardous operations. Their strong commitment to selfless help has meant they have become an Australian icon. Help is born at the moment danger threatens. This is the most efficient kind of help, help at its best.

Helping wildlife has become an obligation as urban developments impinge on wildlife territory. Fortunately, the majority of people in Australia support protection measures for animals in general. The RSPCA (Royal Society for the Prevention of Cruelty to Animals) is an Australia-wide organisation, which operates largely on voluntary participation from communities. It helps all animals, pets as well as wildlife, when danger threatens their natural well-being, their accustomed environment or their very existence. Laws have regulated minimum respect towards other life forms for over one hundred years of the organisation's existence.

Road users, for instance, are urged under the law to avoid driving over wildlife, whether it is a lizard or snake soaking up the warmth of the bitumen road or our larger native animals such as koalas and kangaroos. In some parts in the north of Australia, this might even be a crocodile as road signs indicate, 'Crocs over the road'. This would occur mainly during night hours when the cooler atmosphere entices warm-blooded creatures into seeking the remaining day's heat on the bitumen road. Wildlife on the road, which has been injured by traffic, is equally protected. The aim is to reduce the suffering of all living forms through humane efforts.

Other aid organisations, especially non-profit ones, are a reflection on society's conscience about helping to meet the shortfalls of government help. As we can never reach complete perfection in what we do, it is vital that people share in aid efforts to help top-up what otherwise would be missing. More equality in taking responsibility for each other is the first requirement for offering unconditional help. However, it also needs to be said that help should not be something that is received on a long-term ongoing basis. This would make recipients long-term dependants instead of resurrecting the individual's will to help him/herself.

In the end, everybody has to learn to 'walk the walk' on their own if they are not to add to a community's burden. It is also not a new concept that aid efforts have failed to meet their target because of a vision lacking the essential aspect of building the individual's need to help themselves as much as possible. Throwing money at a problem usually helps score political points but this type of help is often only a short-term quick fix. All that has then been achieved is to run busily around in circles not fixing anything long-term.

How the long-term solution to such problems can be achieved is fortunately well known but less successfully practised. Most of the time, 'help' is falling behind, trying to catch up with the needs of various sections of society. Help is the mortar between building blocks, which come loose without it. The best help is given in a mutual building process where the combined 'mortar' of self-help and charity is placed in time.

If help is seen as the mortar, then the bricks have to be laid in conjunction. A practical example of this is the growing problem of hunger. People deprived of enough food are best helped through a number of necessary steps. The first step is direct assistance in order to meet the immediate pressing need. This creates the preconditions for the recipients to make use of the next step. Supply of basic tools as a second step can prepare further conditions that free them gradually from total dependence on others. If dependence remains in place, help will degenerate into anticipation of total support, which is then taken for granted.

The first step of supplementing food intake will allow people to gain the necessary energy to be guided into achieving a more self-help based model. Local knowledge of the environmental issues can be used for selecting a sustainable area for cultivating a crop. The ancient companion-planting model of the Incas sees a variety of seeds and seedlings planted together. In this way, the plants can support each other. For instance, maize, manioc, tomato, garlic, onions, wheat, cabbage, taro, and beans are all grown together. The alternative monoculture model sees large cleared areas given over to a single crop rather than the multiple smaller pockets surrounded by hedge-plantations of specific fruit.

Companion-planting yield is also much higher than current, widely used monocultures. This was still evident in the remote Inca-Andes settlements of Chile, Peru and Ecuador as recently as 1978 when I happened to be there . Pest control, soil regeneration, environmental responses are natural facts of companion planting and not forced environmental changes.

Another vital step towards self-help is the supplying of tools, which can support better methods of planting and individual maintenance of all life situations. Even a little surplus in the first mutual help steps is a starting-point for more independence when exchanged with other goods of a progressive need. Such a small-cell development is in stark contrast to so - called economical methods of crop cultivation in monoculture.

In America for instance, farmers experience the devastating effects of their large-scale monoculture in crops with climate extremes on an unstoppable scale. The economic benefits of large-scale monoculture in agriculture are still preventing a better insight into other options. The much higher yield of companion planting would justify both targets, more food for the small community as well as more practical employment through intense cultivation. At the same time, it encourages better environmental management.

The capital dependency of large area monocultivation is the barrier stopping the majority of dependant individuals reaching greater independence. A classic example has delivered an entrepreneur of Bangladesh by supporting with very little capital small, private initiatives. Out of experience, women were entrusted with small loans, which they showed could reinforce them as family-carers that are more responsible. They managed to make the small contributions go a long way towards improving their living conditions. What this demonstrates is how a little can achieve a lot if help is handed to the right people in need.

This model of a 'Micro-Business Development' became a worldwide model of self-help starting in Bangladesh. It attracted the Nobel Peace Prize in 2006 for its originator, Muhammad Yunus and included his private initiative, the 'Grameen Banking System'. This was a method of helping people with no creditworthiness to help themselves out of the poverty trap. This is living proof of how individuals who connect to a plan such as this can carry it further simply by applying individually revived efforts. As little as one hundred dollars has helped move people out of an underprivileged, miserable life into a responsible, minutely detailed management plan. For instance, part of the money bought a goat, which one of the children leads daily to a nearby pasture. Keeping a watchful eye on this new possession ensures that the goat can deliver healthy goat's milk when returned home at the end of a day.

In exchange for some of the milk they could give away, they acquired a small amount of textile material which, when sewed skilfully into something useful, continued to add value to the initial investment. An increased return is guaranteed as long as something is added to it at each new stage. An exchange that is made without adding new value can reverse the beneficial increase.

In this process, everything begins with a small input of either funds and/or practical materials. Proper tools, for instance, are vital in helping to meet the goal of an increase in expectations. A proverb says, 'an axe in the right hand can save a carpenter.' It is not just help for the needy, but any helping hand extended to somebody in order to bridge a gap in shortcomings, works with cooperation, too. No cooperation means that any help offered becomes wasted help. When would we be without help? When efforts do not meet their targets or continue to link people in their efforts with each other.

Another fairytale tells a story which demonstrates the theme 'helping other people' from an educational point of view : a brother and a sister went together to the local fun fair shortly before Christmas. Their parents had given each a coin, admonishing them to keep a close eye on how to use the hard-earned money for a special enjoyment. Arriving on foot at the not too distant fair in the market square, the siblings mixed with other local children. They watched the display in colourful booths like the one especially attracting their attention in which a clown figure had a big open mouth into which money was thrown. The coin that reached the target was to be refunded with double its value. While watching other keen players out of the surrounding crowd, not only children their age but also adults, they noticed a boy off to one side. The boy was dressed shabbily and was also watching the clown as many more coins missed the painted target rather than hit it.

"What would you do if you had a coin?" the siblings asked the boy.

"I would buy bread and milk because I haven't had anything to eat since yesterday."

The siblings, never having heard this before were moved with compassion, handing one of their two coins to this poor boy. Happy shining eyes in the boy's beaming face told the siblings just how much their help was appreciated. Well, at least we didn't lose the coin with the enchanting clown, were the immediate thoughts of the siblings.

The other coin they were keeping for the time being. As they watched how many people were missing the clown mouth with their coin they thought, "There must be a better way of getting something for our money." One of the siblings continued, "At least our first coin could help a child in urgent need."

When the brother and the sister left the fun fair in the town's centre, they met other people. It was only a few days away from Christmas and winter had taken over. Despite the missing white layer of snow over the country, the days were cold under a misty cloud cover. White snowflakes would soon be falling. Everybody wore thick clothes to keep warm against the bitterly cold wind gusts. A young boy on the side of the road, however, was not dressed accordingly. He caught the eye of everybody, causing them passing discomfort. However, only the siblings stopped in front of the boy.

"You must be feeling the cold a lot. Haven't you got an overcoat at least?"

"I wish I had, but I can't do much about it," the boy replied anxiously, all the while keeping his arms hugged together close to the body. Another boy from the passing pedestrians joined in the conversation. He wore more than enough winter clothes to keep warm. Under a heavy coat, the siblings could see a thick, woollen light-blue pullover.

"Could you help out this poor fellow with your coat? You still should keep warm enough with your pullover underneath," suggested the siblings to the new arrival.

He quickly responded, "Not for free, only if I get money for it."

"We've only this one coin left; would you leave your coat with this boy for our coin?"

"It's not much but I'd rather have the coin." And the deal was done. The boy on the side of the road - now with a beautifully thick coat - slowly stood up from his awkward sitting position and, hardly believing his luck, promised not to forget this help. Though offered in a somewhat self-serving way, the real irony became that the richer, now coatless, boy lost his profit further down the road with the clown's mouth denying him any profit. The action of the siblings speaks louder than words but our coatless donor proves 'what goes around comes around' and 'virtue has its own reward.'

Back home the siblings told their parents what they had done with their money. "Are you sure that you have done the right thing? You have been very unselfish, which in today's world is a special virtue not much found anymore amongst people. If you remain strong in your belief, life will also remunerate you over time. Everything we do is cyclical. Once a circle has been started with something good like an offer of help to the needy, the circle will continue with the good returning to you too."

Meanwhile a few days had gone by and the parents went to see other family members in the nearby town. They must have missed the bus or perhaps it was not running due to the snow on the road. This year winter had a relentlessly firm grip of biting cold and heavy snow all over the country, so that a walk on foot became very hazardous. Waiting much longer in the cold made the parents decide to make the trip on foot.

Just when the going got tough, a coach pulled by two horses arrived from behind, whirling up snow in clouds from the road. Slowing down before reaching the pedestrian couple, the driver pulled the horses by the reins, stopping next to them. "Do you want a lift with me? You must be the parents of the children who helped those two poor kids in town the other day. Let's make this journey together quickly and in comfort in the cabin protected from this bitter cold and heavy snow. We'll go to the next town and you won't have to worry how to get there."

"This is really kind of you but how do you know about the story of our kids?"

"Good news travels fast; everybody in town knows about it by now. You can be proud of your whole family."

"Thank you for that. Our two kids will hear this good news from us; God may bless us all." The tour went well for all and later in the day, it was also arranged to return together. Back home, the parents showed their pride in their children by giving each of them one coin again for them to decide what they wanted to do with it. The coins were the savings the parents had made when the free two-way trip was offered by a helping hand.

What goes out comes back and so was the help given to others, returning unexpectedly in a circle to its originators. This is the true nature of 'helping other people.'

CHAPTER 19

Leading the Life of an Egotist

The African adage mentioned earlier, 'If you want to go fast, you go it alone' applies to the 'egotist' as well. 'Going it alone' however, means cutting yourself off from either receiving help or finding someone else who would accept help from an egotist. The whole process of help - supporting each other to overcome the shortcomings of life - is put on hold by the egotist, which makes an existence lonely, even miserable.

There is always a choice - a choice about which side to embark on. As long as outside circumstances do not prevail in preventing an individual's choice, there is always an alternative from which to choose. Lucky is the one who is spared the conflict of choice, who is born into life's privileged directions, of which the 'Simple Life' definitely is one but the 'egotist's life' is not. Why this is so simple is the egotist is the one who makes decisions for his/her own benefit instead of being part of the problem/ solution model of his/her fellow human beings.

Here unity also stands for united strength. Not all of course is glitter here; to exclude individual responsibilities in such a unity increases the likelihood of a dependency on other people. Who now is the egotist? Can he/she hide behind distinct human characters? And if so, what makes an egotist?

THE SIMPLE LIFE

Philosophers like I. Kant (1724-1804), A. Schopenhauer (1788-1860) and S. Freud (1856-1939), have already pondered the egotist's life from a philosophical point of view. However, these understandings are also time-related. Does what held up in the 18th century still hold good in the 21st century? Most of their teachings are, to some degree, still coherent today for those who make the effort to interpret their philosophy. It is not an everyday business for the average citizen, no matter what their background, but it can be done with a pre-defined understanding of philosophy. Here is an attempt to find an understanding with a broader acceptance within the community. Most people do not have the time or the conviction of specialised ways to follow and think of life-realities as the majority of people experience them.

Throughout history and up until quite recent times, the ruling minority of the time supported a more individual-model of creativity. However, today, from about 2000 onwards, a broader, more diverse intellect puts up the questions and wants to find the answers within societies. There is an easy way of explaining some things that again, in retrospect, can deliver the answers for the topic of 'The Simple Life'. The opposite path, the difficult way in life, would be in brooding repeatedly what, in reality, could be close to us and simple or is just mind over matter.

While talking philosophy, it is instrumental to also mention that philosophers like R. Descartes (1596-1650, French), G.W. Leibnitz (1646-1716, German), and J.J. Rousseau (1712-1778, French) have searched for the eternal questions and conclusions surrounding our existence in close contact with nature's realities. Here, we can find again the antagonists in philosophy, 'Idealism' and 'Realism'. Kant described this as the 'school concept' standing for 'Idealism' and the 'Universe concept' for 'Realism', in order to find a 'silver lining' through the complexity of philosophy.

This is only a small window of understanding, opening into the immense philosophy 'building'. It is important to stay grounded and look at realities on which we all exist. Flying high into difficult territory has its downsides with any reality. There is the popular understanding that 'what goes up, must come down again'; the ground is territory that is much more familiar.

Who now is the egotist in a common understanding and how do we meet him? Egotists are amongst us in the flow of mainstream society, found at random. A sharp eye is all that's needed to recognise this. Profiteering speaks best for the many egotists amongst us. Those who abide by the rules within societies only to their own benefit have to find the 'loopholes', which allow such 'middle positions' to exist. This then is the egotist amongst us, managing to stay out of isolation through interaction with other people on the grounds of benefit sharing. However, more than one side has to be satisfied to keep the egotist in the game.

If satisfaction is not mutual, the egotist's middle position becomes isolated from mainstream society. A so-called customer, friend, or relation simply turns away, not responding anymore to the one-sided self-interest of the egotist. In a sense, the path to a 'simple life' is here again impeded because, as an egotist eventually goes it alone, it is not obvious how far to go with reference to the aforementioned African proverb.

'Egotist' is also a character feature inherent in every human to differing degrees. The aspects responsible for this are the trigger-mechanisms of aggressive and/or dominant egotist attitudes. Already, the young child develops a sense of ownership with its first possessions, which are usually toys. Only early education about sharing something with others, not exclusively but within the framework of other character features, has in later life a chance of emerging as an opposition to the egotist's attitudes.

Steering such a course from early life on is vital for a person's ability to socialise. In other words, 'anti-social' is another expression for an egotist. However, if we were all egotists, societies couldn't collaborate socially. Alternatively, if there were no egotists - probably called 'idealists' – the pursuit of a functional society would be difficult. What makes a functional society are the oppositional forces of egotist and selfless helper. 'Help' can be described as the mediator between the shortcomings of 'want' and 'can'. Many people 'want' but many fewer 'can', which is a simplistic perception of a society.

A conclusion about a 'simple life' remains then with the individual, tackling the issues of one's own life while under constant observation of other knowledge sources such as the other people in society. They can offer verbal or written encouragement and recommendations but it is important not to make the mistake of forcing conclusions on other people. There is always some principle or other at stake but everything changes constantly and so do we. Therefore, it is no use trying to cement momentary insight into a distant future. Everything works in steps and needs to be tackled systematically, which again is dependent on the individual.

A short own tale again illustrates the dichotomy of the egotist and the philanthropist and how each deals with different life issues.

The Egotist and the Philanthropist see the World Together:

after years of being close neighbours in the same hamlet, the egotist and the philanthropist decided for a change to see the world together, a world outside their usual limited living area. They also thought they knew enough about each other to make the right decision about such a venture. Their own backyard had become too small and awaited the release of two of its long- established citizens into the wider world. Despite not having talked much to each other, one early morning, right in the middle of summer, the two met in the market place long before the little town came to life.

"Where are we heading and how do we go about it as nobody else is around?" the philanthropist broke the silence.

"I don't worry about the others. They can do what they like as long as I'm all right. Getting out of this place, sooner rather than later, is my only concern now; the early bus will take us to the next city from where our adventure should start. You must agree with me because this is our choice. If we were to walk, we'd never get far," responded the egotist.

"Well, I don't mind taking the bus; the early driver is probably my cousin."

"Then this ought to be our first piece of luck. You can make sure that your cousin gives us a courtesy free ride. You know, that's what family is for," retorted the egotist. Not long after, the bus stopped to pick up the two passengers. "You go first and talk to your cousin."

The early hour of the day was marked by the dominant silence of the past night and the bus driver wasn't yet ready for a chat. The philanthropist only briefly welcomed the bus driver sitting in front of the steering wheel, while exchanging money for his ticket.

"Hey, doesn't family at least get a special deal, and what about a friend like me?" interrupted the egotist from the first step of the open bus door.

"This is not a casino; this is a Transport Company which moves people for a fare. You pay the fare and I'll take care of you. By the way, this is not my bus either. I'm only employed and would rather do the right thing by the company so that I can keep my job," was the bus driver's response.

"I can't believe your cousin is that stubborn. I suppose when you pay, I've got to pay, too."

Later during the trip, other people entered the bus. Meanwhile the egotist couldn't get over the fact that no special deal came their way, arguing no end with the philanthropist while the philanthropist tried to catch a glimpse of the landscape on the horizon in a stunningly sunny day.

"Can you leave just one moment undisturbed for me; the day has many more hours still to go," the philanthropist reminded the egotist. The first leg of their bus trip was barely underway before a quarrel developed between the two. "You can have it your way if you don't like travelling with me; it's entirely your choice. Let good understanding and common sense prevail and remember, we have only just started the tour."

On leaving the bus, the philanthropist didn't mind lending a hand to an elderly woman, carrying her suitcase and engaging in a short conversation about the whereabouts of their hometowns.

The egotist on the other hand, got himself off the bus without a word, standing idle on the side watching and wondering what his companion could possibly have to talk about with an old woman they didn't know.

"When you have finished, we better keep moving," was all the egotist impatiently added after a friendly introduction to the woman.

"We are travelling and therefore we have got all the time we need to experience new people, their views and local venues other than those daily repeated ones of our little home town."

"Forget that! Where do we end up with our own trip if we use up our time listening more to other people than pursuing our goal to see the world?"

"Why are you in such a hurry to miss out from the start? All these little things are what make us enjoy the time away from a daily routine?"

"You can have your 'little things' while I'm going to look more for the big ones."

"Are you suggesting that we had better travel separately and find out later at home who caught the better 'train'?"

"You are probably right; I can't wait to travel faster on my own."

"We are free to make our own decisions. If this is what you really want, go for it; I'm not holding you back."

Instead of pulling together to maintain their plan, the egotist and the philanthropist lost common ground even at such an early stage of their trip. The 'little things' grew in importance all of a sudden within an unfamiliar environment. This temporarily isolated the egotist while the philanthropist remained open to new experiences. In fact, the journey into the wider world continued for the two from then on with each moving in a different direction.

They returned later to their hometown, but at different times. The egotist showed up first after snatching up his world vision like a shortened movie. Back home, everything and everybody had remained familiar so that the egotist's life was set to continue as before, having been interrupted for only a short time.

On the part of the philanthropist, he returned much later to the hometown, after having made many contacts with people during his journey. It was from the people that he learned much about other places so that he was never left on his own to find out about good or bad in other places. He might have seen more of both, good and bad, as people never embark on just one of them. Contrary to the egotist, who mainly looked around in order to find confirmation of his own views, the philanthropist experienced with people the rich diversity in the world.

It is often unnoticed that other people guide one's own life-path if one acknowledges a need to connect to them. Such a joint journey through life turns out to be a diverse experience. It is only by not cutting short the innumerable little occurrences in life that one can truly enjoy the 'big' experiences. Back at home, the philanthropist not only continued life as before, but also openly enjoyed sharing his experiences with everybody. He didn't boast about his new experiences, unlike the egotist, but rather waited until questions were asked while going about life's daily routines like everybody else.

The moral of the story is that the egotist ended up isolating himself more, despite stepping out of his 'shell'. The very core of his being, his character, could neither change nor adjust to new life situations. However, the philanthropist benefited from it because he didn't limit himself in pursuing goals disconnected from other people.

EPILOGUE

When writing, we live with a topic throughout the whole exercise, trying to reach exemplary statements, which can connect reader and author to each other in a mutual desire for better answers to growing problems. In addition, at this end of a written exercise, the question arises: how much updating and new universal understanding has been achieved?

Speaking on my behalf as a writer, I tried diversifying this topic between past, present and future challenges, paving the way for a wider, common understanding of this single topic, 'The Simple Life'. How important such a topic might become in everybody's life, time usually can tell over a lifetime. It is only then that experiences are on hand to compare where one is standing at any given time, on a difficult, an easy or a simple life path.

After all these considerations, what is a 'simple life' and how can we conclude which is simple, too? Is there a recipe or a rule on hand that can get us there? The answer to that certainly is not 'simple' as is outlined in the many previous discussions. 'Simplicity' has to be a result of efforts in upgrading traditional past experiences into a current 'think tank' from where new life directions should derive. It is important not to confuse 'simple' with 'easy'. Because it's 'easy' to throw out what cannot be understood any more.

On the other hand, substituting a past insight with new customs is like a dance on the high wire, leading eventually and with some difficulty across to the other side. Then again, when difficulties have been overcome, only then has 'simplicity' been achieved. No difficulties mean no 'simple life' at the end of the 'tunnel'. Therefore, it is vital to deal with difficulties if we want to reach the other side, 'simplicity'.

More often, however, we will not reach this other side, because it is easily forgotten that only difficulties that have been overcome will reveal 'simplicity'. Then again, what is 'difficult' for one person might be 'easy', if not 'simple', for somebody else depending on individual capability as well as flexibility towards unforeseen circumstances. Absolute rules have never worked for the majority of people; neither are rules pertinent long-term. We have no choice other than to seek that path of a 'simple life' because if we were not to achieve this goal during our lifetime, we certainly would towards the end. We would all turn to 'simplicity' in its complete sense.

So what then is 'simple' in life? 'Simple' can be anything which is, by any individual standard, not 'complex' or 'not difficult'. It has become something, which in life is practised, not just understood, to personal satisfaction with others. Keeping this in mind will lead to a 'simple life' over time. One secret to help in getting there lies in not ignoring others as only they can mirror-like, show our simple, wider acceptance.

Shortcomings in such acceptance feed back to the individual in a wide range of developing 'complexes' - personality disorders such as egotism, laziness, hyperactivity, greed, superficiality, crime, and swindling. These represent one side of an equation, which has been addressed in the course of this context. Anything of this nature will distance the individual from achieving a 'simple life'. On the other side are found the favourable aspects of a 'simple life': philanthropy, diligence, help, generosity, and honesty.

Finally, it needs also to be said that much in life is subject to individual choice and so too can a 'simple life' become an individual's preferred, meaningful choice.

APPENDIX

my special contribution to accompany "The Simple Life"

A Glorious Day
Poem , Martin Kari

Silence still rules over the night.
The moon has travelled its path.
Sitting at the horizon waiting to change over,
Nightlight segues into daylight sun.
The net of little starlight holes in the sky have shown
Distant messages to resting dark Mother Earth.

A new day is born every time the fiery sun
Looks over the bowed, far horizon.
First, in dark blue shimmering haze
Adopted by growing red ribbon-flame walls,
For the first time lightening bush, houses, trees,
Sending their long, dark shades on to wider, spreading ground.
Vanishing, shade creations accompany silence,
Stepping back with time to allow bright orange sunlight
To finally flood all the chosen land
With bright daylight in a piercing yellow disc;
This time through a sky free of barricading clouds,
Now an azure-blue spectacle.

First in the air, a cautious birdsong,
Then on the ground, life begins an almost daily routine
Following a rule that 'The early bird catches the worm.'
People, too, hear this call,
Seemingly moving everything, including themselves,
Into the awakening, morning hours.

Cosy, sunny warmth from the sky
Reconciles with a chilly night,
Eating away foggy mist to prepare a glorious, clear day
More bright sunlight rises into the sky,
More people down on earth.
All society backdrops, rush, rest, drive restless vehicles,
And are driven in numbers by again larger
People-movers in buses, trains,
And further away, even our large 'bird mimics'
Take to the air.

Silence of the night has gone into hiding
Where it is not reached by this daily human hubbub.
It is in nature where we all recharge our 'batteries'
In our oases : forests, wide wilderness, where land meets
A river or the ocean, mountains, closer to city's green,
Blossoming parks, and often in protected
Homey surroundings.

What we prefer doing, most of it we take
Into nature's oases, too.
A far cry from daily pressure, life then
Can worship a glorious day.
Not only our leisure hours
Recognise a glorious day.

Everybody in an office, a workshop,
In the open field, the athlete, the sick, the rich,
The young, the poor, the old,
All enjoy a glorious day.

Past difficult days escape more easily
From our memories,
Giving wings to a new, better hope.
And all this only, because the sun has taken
The reigns of the day,
Shining generously, indiscriminately, quietly,
Onto our lucky spot, Mother Earth.
All we see, all we know, is accidental.
Not to recognise the 'glory' around us,
Especially highlighted by the sun,
Makes life hard in reconciling with poor, sunny days.

Life has never been all sunshine.
We grab the sunny moments of life
Or go down the road of despair.
Day's warmth finally slips into
The first hours of after midday,
Keeping it up for all afternoon,
The sun starts to hover towards
The horizon again, resending
Its longer shadowy creations.

And so do all daily rush-hours follow
Into a calmer evening, preparing
A night silence to return.
The balmy night not yet hints at
The chill to come, while the sun's farewell,

Cooler hours carry a bite in the air,
Sending many of us back into houses
Where artificial lights attempt
To replace the day's sun.

Life carries on slowly, however,
To be taken over by silence,
Sending mainly daylight creatures
To worship a rest time
Upon which the star lights
And the enlightened moon face,
Sent by the sinking sun, keep equal
Vigilance over remaining activities;
Likewise a sleeping world, which
Prepares for another, hopefully glorious day.
Moon, shine on us and let the sun rest too.

www.ingramcontent.com/pod-product-compliance
Lightning Source LLC
Chambersburg PA
CBHW030552080526
44585CB00012B/349